FAMILY CHILD CARE

2018 Tax Companion

Being a Family Child Care Professional

Family child care is a special profession for those who love young children. As a professional family child care provider, you must balance the skills required to care for children with those required to operate your business. Here are some tips that will keep your family child care business as healthy and successful as possible:

- Learn the child care regulations for your area, and follow them.
- Join your local family child care association.
- Sign up with your local child care resource and referral agency.
- Join the Child and Adult Care Food Program (CACFP).
- Find good professional advisers (such as a tax professional, insurance agent, and lawyer).
- Actively participate in training to acquire and improve your professional skills.

Additional Resources

Redleaf Press (www.redleafpress.org; 800-423-8309) publishes resources for family child care professionals. Redleaf Press offers the following publications to support your business:

- Starting a family child care business:
     Family Child Care Business Planning Guide

- Promoting your business:
     Family Child Care Marketing Guide, 2nd edition

- Creating contracts and policies:
     Family Child Care Contracts and Policies, 4th edition
     Sharing in the Caring: Agreement Packet for Parents and Providers
     The Redleaf Complete Forms Kit for Both Family Child Care and Center-Based Programs, Revised edition

- Keeping accurate records and filing your taxes:
     Family Child Care Record-Keeping Guide, 9th edition
     The Redleaf Calendar-Keeper: A Record-Keeping System for Family Child Care Professionals
     Family Child Care Tax Workbook and Organizer
     Family Child Care Tax Companion

- Reducing your business risks:
     Family Child Care Legal and Insurance Guide

- Managing your money and planning for retirement:
     Family Child Care Money Management and Retirement Guide

FAMILY CHILD CARE

2018 Tax Companion

TOM COPELAND, JD

Redleaf Press®
www.redleafpress.org
800-423-8309

Tom Copeland is a licensed attorney and has conducted tax workshops for family child care providers since 1982. In 2017, his website (www.tomcopelandblog.com) was chosen as one of the Top 75 Childcare Blogs and Websites for Childcare Providers and Parents by Feedspot (ranked second in the United States). In 2014, his blog (www.tomcopelandblog.com) was chosen as one of the top 50 money management blogs in the country by Direct Capital, a national financing company. In 1998, he won the Child Care Advocate of the Year award from the Minnesota Licensed Family Child Care Association. In 2003, he received the Friend of the National Association for Family Child Care (NAFCC) award from NAFCC. In 2004, Tom received the Advocate of the Year award from NAFCC. Tom is the author of *Family Child Care Business Planning Guide*, *Family Child Care Contracts and Policies*, *Family Child Care Legal and Insurance Guide* (with Mari Millard), *Family Child Care Marketing Guide*, *Family Child Care Money Management and Retirement Guide*, *Family Child Care Record-Keeping Guide*, and *Family Child Care Tax Workbook and Organizer*. These publications are available from Redleaf Press. Tom Copeland can be reached by email at tomcopeland@live.com, by phone at 651-280-5991, or through his website at www.tomcopelandblog.com.

Published by Redleaf Press
10 Yorkton Court
St. Paul, MN 55117
www.redleafpress.org

Cover design by Jim Handrigan
Cover photograph © iStockphoto.com/Andrea Manciu
Typeset in Times
Printed in the United States of America
ISBN 978-1-60554-649-0
Printed on acid-free paper

FSC
www.fsc.org
MIX
Paper from
responsible sources
FSC® C011935

DISCLAIMER
This publication is designed to provide accurate information about filing federal tax returns for family child care providers. Tax laws, however, are in a constant state of change, and errors and omissions may occur in this text. We are selling this publication with the understanding that neither Redleaf Press nor the author is engaged in rendering legal, accounting, or other professional services. If you require expert legal or tax assistance, obtain the services of a qualified professional. Because each tax return has unique circumstances, neither the author nor Redleaf Press guarantees that following the instructions in this publication will ensure that your tax return is accurate or will enable you to find all the errors on your tax return. In addition, this book addresses only tax issues related to family child care. This publication is to be used for filling out 2018 tax forms only. For information on how to fill out tax forms after 2018, please consult later editions of this publication.

Contents

Acknowledgments

Thanks to the following tax professionals and family child care providers who reviewed and commented on early drafts of this book. Their feedback was extremely helpful. Tax professionals: Sandy Schroeder, Meredith Coghlan, Michael Eisenberg, Sue Knie, Lori J. Salati, R. Mike Flint, Normand Marchessault, Kelly Nokleby, Laura Strombom, Doyle Pendleton, Glen Barker, Barbara DelBene, Stephen Sacco, Pat Gathe, Kathy Whynott, and Don Gilbo. Family child care providers: Gayle Sarkissian, Laurie Ann Meyer, Susan Morgan, Dayvetta Jordan, Ruth VonWald, Judith Behrens, and Dawn Abel. Thanks to Douglas Schmitz for his editorial help.

If you have comments about how this book might be improved for later editions, please contact Tom Copeland by email at tomcopeland@live.com, by phone at 651-280-5991, or through his website at www.tomcopelandblog.com.

What's New for This Tax Year

- 2018 saw a number of significant changes in tax laws affecting family child care providers. Here are the top two:

  ○ Family child care providers may now deduct in one year (rather than depreciating) any item, regardless of its cost. The exceptions to this rule are the purchase of a home, home improvement, or a home addition. See page 28 for details.

  ○ Providers can reduce their federal taxable income by subtracting 20% of their profit or their family's taxable income, whichever is smaller. For example, if a married provider had a business profit of $30,000 and her family's taxable income was $50,000, she could reduce her federal taxable income by $6,000 ($30,000 x 20% = $6,000). This rule does not affect the amount owed by providers for Social Security and Medicare taxes or state income taxes. See the *2018 Family Child Care Tax Workbook and Organizer* for details.

- Although the corporate tax rate drops substantially to 21% in 2018, it still doesn't make sense for most providers to incorporate to get this lower rate. Talk to a tax professional and a lawyer before operating other than as a sole proprietor (self-employed). For more on this subject, see my *Family Child Care Legal and Insurance Guide.*

- The standard meal allowance rates for 2018 are $1.31 breakfast, $2.46 for lunch and supper, and $0.73 for snacks. The rates are higher for Alaska and Hawaii.

- The standard mileage rate for 2018 is $0.545 per business mile.

- The income eligibility limits for the Earned Income Credit have increased to $46,100 (for married couples filing jointly with one child) and $40,320 (if single with one child).

- The income limits to qualify for the IRS Saver's Credit has increased to $63,000 (adjusted gross income) for couples filing jointly; $47,250 for heads of household; and $31,500 for individuals or married people filing separately.

For more information on tax changes, see the *Family Child Care 2018 Tax Workbook and Organizer*. For copies of all IRS tax forms and instructions, go to www.irs.gov.

Introduction

This book is designed for family child care providers who are working with a tax professional or who would like to do so. It includes suggestions for finding and choosing a tax professional, an organizer that will make providing information to your tax professional easier, and checklists to help you review your tax forms before submitting them. This book will also help your tax professional understand the special tax rules that apply to family child care businesses and take advantage of all the business deductions that you're entitled to claim.

This book has two parts: Part 1 can help you locate a qualified tax professional and determine if he is familiar with the special tax rules for family child care. Part 1 also explains how to go about resolving any questions or disagreements that may arise when working with your tax professional. Part 2 is the Tax Organizer. It provides clear, detailed instructions for gathering and calculating the information that your tax professional will need to complete your business tax forms, including **Form 8829**, **Form 4562**, and **Schedule C**. It also includes a review checklist for each of these tax forms so you can easily double-check them and discuss any questions with your preparer.

The organizer can help save you money by ensuring that you pay only the taxes that you owe. It can also reduce your stress by making it easier to gather the information for your tax professional and by helping you feel more confident that your tax professional is filling out your tax return accurately.

You can use this book if you meet your state's child care regulations or are exempt from them, as long as you file your tax returns as a sole proprietor (self-employed person) or as a single-person limited liability company (LLC). If you file as a partnership or a corporation, you must file different tax forms and follow different tax rules than those described here.

Licensing Status and Tax Rules

You can take advantage of the tax rules described in this book based on your licensing status as a family child care provider. If you meet your state's child care licensing rules, you are entitled to claim all of the deductions associated with your home and business described in this book. If you are exempt from your state's child care licensing rules, you are entitled to claim the same deductions as if you were licensed. Let's say, for example, that your state requires you to have a license if you care for children from more than one family. If you care for children from only one family, you are exempt from licensing rules and are entitled to claim the same deductions as if you were licensed.

If you are in violation of your state's child care licensing rules, you are not entitled to claim business expenses associated with your home, such as your property tax, mortgage interest, utilities, house repairs, homeowners insurance, and house depreciation. You can still deduct all other business expenses, such as food, toys, supplies, depreciation on furniture and appliances, car expenses, and so on. If you are operating illegally but have applied to be licensed before the end of the year, you can deduct expenses as if you were licensed as long as your application has not been denied.

Record-Keeping and Tax Preparation Tools

This book is part of an integrated set of books and other tools that provide a complete record-keeping and tax preparation system for family child care providers. Here's an introduction to the tools and how they work together.

Keeping Your Records

- The *Family Child Care Record-Keeping Guide* will help you learn about the business records that you need to keep and help you identify over 1,000 deductions for your business.

- The *Redleaf Calendar-Keeper*, *Mileage-Keeper*, *Business Receipt Book*, and *Inventory-Keeper* will help you track your income, expenses, payments, and depreciable property.

Preparing Your Taxes

- **Method 1**: Do your own taxes. Use the *Family Child Care Tax Workbook and Organizer* for the current tax year. It includes a Tax Organizer with detailed instructions for filling out your tax forms and many examples; it also includes blank tax forms that you can tear out and copy.

- **Method 2**: Hire a tax professional. Use the *Family Child Care Tax Companion* for the current tax year to help you find and work with a tax professional, gather and organize the information she will need, and double-check your return before it is submitted.

Part 1: Working with a Tax Professional

If you're reading this book, you're probably already working with a tax professional or seriously considering taking that step. If you have been doing your taxes yourself, hiring a tax professional can feel like a big step. The suggestions in this part of the book will help you choose the right person and work with her most effectively. You may also be wondering whether tax preparation software, such as TurboTax or H&R Block, is a viable alternative to hiring a tax professional. So before discussing how to go about finding a good tax professional, let's review the pros and cons of using tax software.

Should You Use Tax Preparation Software?

An increasing number of family child care providers are using tax preparation software to do their own taxes. These programs can help with math calculations (such as depreciation) and completing your tax forms; they may also help catch some of your mistakes, but they also have drawbacks. Specifically, tax software *will not* do the following:

- Identify the items you can deduct for your business. The software will merely list the category on each line (for example, "Supplies"); it will be up to you to figure out what you can claim on that line.

- Explain how to deduct items that are used both for business and personal purposes. You will need to figure out how to claim not only the supplies you use exclusively for business but also those you use for both business and personal purposes.

- Alert you to all the special rules that apply to your business. For example, it won't remind you that the Food Program reimbursements you received for your own children are not taxable income.

- Ask you detailed questions to make sure you are reporting the highest Time-Space percentage and business deductions you are allowed to claim.

Unlike software, a tax professional who is familiar with the special rules for your business should be able to help you with all of the above issues. Because of these and other weaknesses (software programs can contain errors), I don't recommend you use tax preparation software unless you already have a good understanding of all the tax rules that apply to family child care businesses. (If you do use tax software, be sure to read the *Record-Keeping Guide* to identify all the allowable deductions for your business and the latest *Tax Workbook and Organizer* to make sure you are following current tax rules.) Look for extensive reviews of tax software programs (TurboTax, H&R Block, and TaxAct) on my website: www.tomcopelandblog.com.

Locating Tax Professionals in Your Area

Once you make the decision to work with a tax professional, the next step is finding the right person. First of all, it's extremely important that your tax professional understand the special tax rules that apply to family child care businesses. Here are some suggestions to help you find a tax professional who is familiar with your type of business:

- The National Association for Family Child Care (NAFCC) has posted a tax preparer directory on its website (www.nafcc.org). It is somewhat outdated but it lists preparers who do family child care tax returns. It is available only to members.

- Contact one of the three national tax organizations that offer state listings of their professional members: the National Association of Enrolled Agents (www.naea.org or 202-822-6232), the National Association of Tax Professionals (www.natptax.com or 800-558-3402), or the National Society of Accountants (www.nsacct.org or 800-966-6679). You can also look in the phone book for the local chapter of any of these organizations.

- Ask other family child care providers or members of your family child care association if they can recommend a good tax professional in your area.

- Call the IRS at 800-906-9887 to find out if there is an IRS Volunteer Income Tax Assistance (VITA) site close to you. This program offers free tax help for taxpayers with household incomes under $50,000. VITA volunteers are trained to help prepare basic tax returns in sites across the country. Since some VITA sites don't prepare business tax returns, be sure to first ask if a site prepares returns for family child care businesses.

- Find out if there are any community tax resources that you are qualified to use. For example, some communities have taxpayer assistance services for low-income people. For more information about these programs, contact your local United Way.

You might also be considering a commercial tax preparation agency; however, most of these businesses focus primarily on tax returns for wage earners rather than home-based businesses. In addition, a tax professional at one of these agencies may be unfamiliar with the unique tax rules that apply to family child care. If you're considering a tax preparation service, ask whether the person who will be doing your return has had any recent training on tax returns for home-based businesses—and be prepared to explain the tax rules for family child care to your preparer.

Check Credentials

By following the above suggestions, you will probably be able to collect the names of at least a few tax professionals. Because of the nature of your business, you can't necessarily assume that any experienced tax professional will be able to prepare your return correctly. Once you have collected your referrals, the next step is to ask each professional about his training and credentials. Ideally, you are looking for someone who is an enrolled agent (EA):

- An EA has earned this credential from the IRS by passing a test in tax preparation.

- A certified public accountant (CPA) is less likely to be familiar with family child care taxes than is an EA.

- A tax attorney or tax professional who specializes in family child care returns may be a good choice if the person is very familiar with the field and has kept up with the annual changes in tax laws.

An EA, CPA, or lawyer can represent you before the IRS if you are audited. Tax professionals who lack these credentials usually cannot.

Conduct Interviews

Once you narrow your referrals to the tax professionals who have the credentials you are looking for, the next step is to determine how familiar each person is with the tax rules involved in your business.

First, ask about the preparer's experience doing family child care returns:

- How many family child care tax returns did the tax professional complete last year? Although experience is important, a less-experienced preparer may have more motivation to learn about your business and keep up with changes in the tax law.

- Of the family child care tax returns that the tax professional signed, how many have been audited over the years? Was the preparer at fault in any of those audits? Although being audited is not necessarily a reflection of the tax professional's skill (many audits are chosen at random), you will want to find out if the preparer did the returns correctly.

Next, find out if the preparer is familiar with the following issues that are specific to family child care businesses:

- **Calculating the business use of your home and your Time-Space percentage**. The preparer should know that you are entitled to include all the hours that you have worked, even after the children are gone.

- **Reporting Food Program income and expenses and the IRS standard meal allowance rate**. The preparer should know the current meal rates and should remind you to count meals that weren't reimbursed by the Food Program when using those rates to figure your food expenses.

- **Depreciating household furniture, equipment, and appliances that are used in your business, and home depreciation**. The preparer should know that you are entitled to claim this depreciation and that it is always worthwhile to do so.

- **Paying employees**. The preparer should know that you need to withhold and pay Social Security taxes (and perhaps state employment taxes) on your payments to anyone who helps you care for the children, no matter how small the amount. Exceptions to this rule are rare.

You are responsible for any mistakes on your tax return, even if a mistake is made by your tax professional. (You also need to keep the proper records to support the numbers on your tax forms.) The Tax Organizer in part 2 of this book will help you communicate with your tax professional and will help you and your tax professional avoid the most common mistakes on family child care tax forms.

Hire the Best Person

Once you have narrowed your list to the professionals who have the credentials you are looking for and who understand the special rules that apply to your business, it's time to choose the best person. In making this decision, consider the following questions:

- Is the tax professional available all year or only during the tax season? Does the preparer do tax planning for the upcoming year? A tax professional who is in business year-round and who does tax planning will probably be able to offer you better service.

- What does the tax professional charge? Is the fee based on a flat amount per return, a charge per form, or an hourly rate? Some tax professionals will quote a range before looking at your particular situation. Be sure to ask up front about all the fees.

- Is the tax professional willing to provide references from other clients who are family child care providers? Ask the clients if the tax professional returned their calls promptly, was easy to work with, and answered all their questions.

- Do you and the tax professional share a similar philosophy about taxes? If you are very conservative in claiming deductions, look for a professional who understands this and will follow your wishes. If you are more assertive in claiming deductions, look for someone who is comfortable with this approach.

- Do you feel comfortable with the tax professional? Is the person easy to reach and to talk with?

Working with Your Tax Professional

When you choose a tax professional, show her the Tax Organizer in part 2 of this book. Some tax professionals have their own tax worksheets or organizers that they like their clients to use. The advantage of the organizer in this book is that it is specifically designed for family child care providers, and your tax professional will probably find it helpful. Before you fill it out, however, show it to your preparer and find out if she has any concerns about using it. Also ask for a list of the other information and records that she will need from you. For example, your tax professional is likely to ask for the following:

- a copy of your last tax return
- any estimated tax payments you made this year
- any **Form 1099**s you received
- any **W-2** forms you or your spouse received
- any other income you received

The next step is to fill out the Tax Organizer and send it to your tax professional. The information in this section is organized by tax form to make it easy for you to fill out and convenient for your tax professional to use. The notes and checklists will help alert both you and your tax professional to the special rules that apply to family child care, so you can both ensure that your taxes are accurate and take advantage of all the deductions you are entitled to claim.

Review Your Return

After your tax professional completes your tax forms, use the checklists in the Tax Organizer to review them, comparing each line to the numbers in your organizer. It's important to ask questions and make sure that you understand every line on your tax forms. In particular, make sure that all the income and deductions you entered in the Tax Organizer appear on your tax forms. If you have any concerns, raise them with your tax professional before you sign your return.

Discuss Any Disagreements

If you and your tax professional have a disagreement, or if her recommendations run counter to those in this book, first ask for an explanation. There may be more than one correct way to handle a particular issue. You may not have understood the tax rules correctly, you may have forgotten something, or your tax professional may have made an error. Most disagreements are likely to be misunderstandings that can be resolved with a brief discussion.

If you continue to disagree, don't just rely on your tax professional's word. Ask her to show you a written authority that supports her position. That authority may be the IRS Tax Code, an IRS publication, a Tax Court case, a Revenue Ruling, or some other IRS document.

For example, let's say that you have always counted the hours you spend attending training workshops as part of your Time-Space percentage on **Form 8829**, and now your tax professional says that you can't do that. So you ask, "Where does it say that I can't count these hours?" She will show you line 4 on **Form 8829**, which refers to the hours that the home is used for child care. When you are away from your home, even on a business activity, you aren't using your home for business. It's logical to conclude that activities away from home do not constitute business use of your home.

Seek Outside Help

If your tax professional can't produce a written authority for her position, look elsewhere for documentation. (If you can find it, be sure to share it with your tax professional so that you can both learn about the point in dispute.) In this situation, there are resources that you can consult:

- **The IRS**. Call them (800-829-4933), ask your question, and request a written authority for the answer. For example, you and your tax professional disagree about whether you can claim a portion of your car loan interest when you use the standard mileage rate. You ask the IRS, "May I deduct the business portion of my car loan interest if I'm using the standard mileage rate to claim my car expenses? Please cite written documentation for your answer." The agent should point out the section on the standard mileage rate in IRS **Publication 463 Travel, Entertainment, Gift, and Car Expenses** that says, "If you are self-employed and use your car in your business, you can deduct that part of the interest expense that represents your business use of the car."

- **Tom Copeland's website**. I have posted IRS documents that apply to family child care on my website, www.tomcopelandblog.com. I have also posted many articles that might help you find an answer to your specific question.

- **The books in the Redleaf Press business series**. You may also find the answer in Redleaf Press books, especially the *Tax Workbook and Organizer* for the relevant tax year and the *Record-Keeping Guide*. You can order any of these publications from Redleaf Press by calling 800-423-8309 or visiting www.redleafpress.org.

Resolve Differing Interpretations

Sometimes there won't be any written documentation for a point you are disputing with your tax professional. For example, there is no written authority that specifically states whether your toothpaste, your garden hose, or the service contract on your refrigerator is deductible. The best documentation you might be able to find is the Tax Code, section 162(a), which says that expenses that are "ordinary and necessary" in your business are deductible. This may leave you arguing with your tax professional about whether the item that you want to deduct really is "ordinary and necessary" to your business or not.

When there is no definitive answer, there's no simple answer to differing interpretations. After discussing this with your tax professional, you may decide to rely on her judgment—or your tax professional may agree to do it your way.

Remember that in the end, you are the one who is responsible for what is on your tax return. If the IRS audits you and denies any of the deductions you have claimed, it is you—not your tax professional—who will have to pay any extra taxes and penalties that may be due.

Where Does It Say That? IRS Authorities on Unique Family Child Care Tax Issues

There are a number of tax issues that are mostly unique to family child care providers. I've posed these issues in the form of statements below. For each statement I've cited IRS documents that support the statement. These IRS authorities include IRS publications, Tax Court cases, and other documents. I've also included some of my experiences in representing family child care providers in IRS audits over the past 30 years, which includes six U.S. Tax Court cases that I have won.

You can use this information to educate yourself and your tax preparer about what to put on your tax return. If your tax preparer does not believe that any one of the statements below is true, ask, "Where does it say that?" You want to know what written authority your tax preparer is using to support a position that is different from my statements below. If he can't show you something in writing, you should feel confident that the statements below are correct.

Warning: Despite these IRS documents and my many years of experience representing family child care providers in IRS audits, there is no absolute guarantee that the statements I make below will be accepted in your IRS audit. This can be for several reasons. One: New IRS Tax Court cases and changes in the law can reverse these statements. Two: Individual IRS auditors may have their own interpretations of the law or may ignore the authorities cited below. Auditors are not required to accept the decisions of other Tax Court cases.

However, you can use the document citations below in conversations with your tax preparer or auditor to make a pretty persuasive case in your defense by saying, "Here is an IRS document that supports my position. What other IRS documents exist that say something different? If there is no other document, then I believe I am entitled to my position. I reasonably followed this document, and I should be allowed to claim what is on my tax return." In my experience, using this approach will almost always be successful.

The most important IRS document for family child care providers is the **Child Care Providers Audit Technique Guide (Audit Guide)**. The IRS revised it in 2009. This publication is used by IRS auditors to educate them about the business of family child care. It contains many helpful statements that can be used to resolve disputes. I've written a commentary about this guide here: http://tinyurl.com/h7mwtbn.

The citations for all IRS authorities are listed at the end of this section.

Child and Adult Care Food Program

Reimbursements from the Food Program for Child Care Children Are Taxable Income

The **Audit Guide** says, "If the provider receives reimbursement for food costs through the CACFP . . . or any other program, the provider can report all the reimbursements under the income section of Part I of the **Schedule C** and then deduct the food expenses in full, which is the recommended method especially when the provider receives a **Form 1099** from the program, or the provider can net the amount reimbursed against the food expense. If the provider uses the netting method and the food expense is greater than the reimbursement, then the provider may deduct the excess as a food expense. If the reimbursements exceed the total food expenses, then the provider should report the excess income in Part I on the **Schedule C**. The netting method is not a preferred method since an Examiner will always be looking for the food reimbursement amounts."

The netting method is described in IRS **Publication 587 Business Use of Your Home**, although the language of the **Audit Guide** is more authoritative.

In every audit I have been involved with in the last 30 years, the auditor wanted to see Food Program reimbursements reported as income. Don't use the netting method.

Reimbursements from the Food Program for Your Own Children Are Not Taxable Income

The **Audit Guide** says, "The provider should not include the amount of the payments for his/her own children because it is not taxable."

IRS **Publication 587 Business Use of Your Home** says, "Do not include payments or expenses [of food] for your own children if they are eligible for the program [Food Program]. Follow this procedure even if you receive a **Form 1099-MISC**, Miscellaneous Income, reporting a payment from the sponsor."

You Are Entitled to Deduct All Meals and Snacks You Serve to Children, Even Those That Are Not Reimbursed by the Food Program

IRS **Rev. Proc. 2003-22** says, "The rates [standard meal allowance rate] apply regardless of whether a family day care provider is reimbursed for food costs, in whole or in part, under the CACFP, or under any other program, for a particular meal or snack."

The **Audit Guide** says, "The provider may use the standard meal and snack rate for a maximum of one breakfast, one lunch, one dinner, and three snacks per eligible child per day."

You Are Entitled to Deduct Food Expenses Using the Standard Meal and Snack Method Whether or Not You Are on the Food Program or Are Licensed

The **Audit Guide** says, "The revenue procedure [**Rev. Proc. 2003-22**] applies to any family day care provider whether or not the provider received reimbursements under the CACFP or is registered, licensed, or regulated by the state in which it operates."

Time-Space Percentage

You Can Count a Room as Being Regularly Used for Your Business If the Business Use Is Continuous, Ongoing, or Recurring

The Uphus and Walker Tax Court cases say, "We have found that regular basis test is met where the taxpayer is able to establish that the business use is continuous, ongoing, or recurring."

IRS Revenue Ruling 92-3 says, "If a room is available for day care use throughout each business day and is regularly used as a part of A's routine provision of day care (including a bathroom, an eating area for meals, or a bedroom used for naps), the square footage of that room will be considered as used for day care throughout each business day. A day care provider is not required to keep records of the specific hours of usage of such a room during business hours. Also, the occasional non-use of such a room for a business day will not disqualify the room from being considered regularly used." Similar language is found in IRS **Publication 587 Business Use of Your Home**.

In my experience, if a provider can show that she uses a room two to three times a week, this will be accepted as regular use.

You Must Count the Basement and Garage as Part of the Total Square Footage of Your Home

The **Audit Guide** says, "The basement square footage must be added to the total square footage. Another common error occurs in cases where the taxpayer is using the garage in the business. You must be sure that the square footage of the garage is added to the denominator (total home space) as well as the numerator (business usage space)."

In my experience the vast majority of providers are regularly using their garage and basement for their business. See the Uphus and Walker cases for guidance in what constitutes regular use of a garage.

You Can Count Hours Spent on Business Activities in Your Home When Children Are Not Present

The **Audit Guide** says, "Hours spent cooking, cleaning, and preparing activities for the business of child care could be included in the calculation of the numerator of the time percentage."

The **Audit Guide** also indicates that hours spent on such activities could be counted if done on weekends and that business record-keeping time can be counted.

IRS Revenue Ruling 92-3 allowed a provider to claim one half hour a day before and after the children were present spent on preparing for and cleaning up after the children.

The Neilson Tax Court case allowed two hours each morning "organizing the facility and preparing luncheon meals for the children," and about one hour each evening after the children departed for "cleaning and reorganizing the day-care facility."

A letter from the Acting Assistant Chief Counsel of the IRS says, "Hours spent cooking, cleaning, and preparing activities for the business of child care could be included in the calculation of the Time-Space percentage if the tests for deduction under section 162 of the code are otherwise met under the facts of the particular case."

Children Do Not Have to Be in a Room for It to Be Counted as Regularly Used for Your Business

The Uphus Tax Court case found that a provider used her laundry room and storage areas on a regular basis, even though children did not regularly use the rooms. "The fact that the children were generally not allowed in the areas is not dispositive of the issue. The issue is whether the area in question is regularly used in the operation of the taxpayer's day-care business, not whether or not the children are present in that area."

You Can Have an Exclusive-Use Room Even if It's Not Separated by a Wall or Partition

The Hewett Tax Court case allowed a taxpayer to claim an exclusive-use area for a piano in a living room. The court said that it wasn't necessary to have a physical barrier to prove that an area was used exclusively for business.

Many providers have an open basement area with a playroom and a washer/dryer/furnace area. They could count the play area as exclusive space without a physical barrier separating it from the washer/dryer/furnace area.

You Can Walk through an Exclusive-Use Room to Get to Another Room and Not Destroy Its Exclusivity

The Miller Tax Court case allowed a taxpayer to claim an exclusive-use room even though she walked through it to get to her bedroom.

The Rayden Tax Court case allowed an exclusive-use room even though visitors to the home walked through it on occasion.

Your Time-Space Percentage Can Be Above 50%

The Neilson Tax Court case allowed a 54% Time-Space percentage because the provider spent three hours each weekday on activities when children were not present, and she occasionally provided child care on weekends.

I have won two Tax Court cases in which one provider won a Time-Space percentage of 93% and the other 98%. In both cases, the provider cared for children 24 hours a day, 7 days a week. The only issue was whether the provider could prove that children were present in her home for these days and hours. Since these two cases were settled before they went before a judge, they are not published opinions, and cannot be cited as authorities in other audits. However, providers should feel comfortable claiming such long hours if they can show the proper records (sign in/out sheets, attendance, or Food Program records). I have won other IRS audits where providers had exclusive use rooms that increased their Time-Space percentage above 50%. Don't let anyone tell you there is an upper limit to your Time-Space percentage that you should not exceed.

You Can Have One or More Exclusive-Use Rooms in Your Home as Well as Regular-Use Rooms

The **Audit Guide** says, "A provider may have a combination of exclusively used rooms and regular used rooms."

The Instructions to IRS **Form 8829 Business Use of Your Home** provides the formula for how to calculate your Time-Space percentage when you have an exclusive-use room and a regular-use room.

Depreciation

You Do Not Have to Have a Child Care License to Be Able to Claim Depreciation on Your Home

To claim house expenses, Internal Revenue Tax Code Section 280A(c)(4)(B) says, "The provider must have applied for, been granted, or be exempt from having a license, certification, registration, or approval as a day care center or as a family or group day care home under state law." This language is repeated in the **Audit Guide** and in IRS **Publication 587 Business Use of Your Home**.

You Are Always Better Off if You Depreciate Your Home

Some tax preparers and providers believe that you should not depreciate your home because you will have to pay higher taxes when you sell your home. In fact, you will owe taxes on the amount of depreciation you claimed, or were entitled to claim, when you sell your home.

IRS **Publication 587** says, "If you were entitled to deduct depreciation on the part of your home used for business, you cannot exclude the part of the gain equal to any depreciation you deducted (or could have deducted) for periods after May 6, 1997."

The **Audit Guide** says, "Therefore, a provider/owner who used part of his or her home for business purposes may not exclude any gain from the sale of that residence that is attributable to depreciation adjustments taken or allowed for periods after May 6, 1997."

You Can Depreciate Household Items You Owned Before You Went into Business

The **Audit Guide** says, "For many providers, when they start their business, many items which were personal use only are used in the business. They are entitled to depreciate the business use portion of those assets. . . . The fact that the asset was only used for personal purposes prior to being placed in service does not disqualify it from being converted to use in the business."

Deductions

You Can Deduct the Business Portion of Your Cable Television Bill

The Simpson Tax Court case recognized that cable television can be deducted as a utility expense on IRS **Form 8829 Expenses for Business Use of Your Home**.

You Can Deduct Lawn Care Expenses

The **Audit Guide** specifically mentions lawn expenses as being deductible.

IRS Tax Court case *Robert and Dorothy Neilson v. Commissioner* (Tax Court Decision 94-1, 1990) allows the Time-Space percentage of lawn care expenses.

You Can Deduct Common Household Items

The **Audit Guide** specifically cites toys, laundry facilities, soap, computers, office equipment, kitchen equipment, playground equipment, furniture, appliances, pianos, VCRs, televisions, stereos, camcorders, diapers, office supplies, cleaning supplies, and educational and art supplies as deductible business expenses.

IRS **Publication 587 Business Use of Your Home** lists "non-food supplies used for food preparation, service, or storage, such as containers, paper produces, or utensils" as expenses that can be deducted.

Just because an item isn't specifically mentioned in these publications doesn't mean it can't be deducted. Providers are entitled to deduct all "ordinary and necessary" business expenses.

Items Can Be Deducted That Are Not Used 100% for Your Business

The **Audit Guide** says, "It is important to stress the fact that having a personal usage element present does not disqualify the property from being a deductible IRC Section 162 expense." Internal Revenue Tax Code Section 162 allows businesses to deduct expenses that are "ordinary and necessary" for their business.

Trips Can Be Claimed as Business Trips Even if They Also Involve Personal Activities

The **Audit Guide** says, "Some trips are obviously primarily for business, while others might be personal or a combination of both. If a taxpayer travels to a single destination and engages in both personal and business activities, the expense is deductible only if the trip is related primarily to the taxpayer's trade or business."

You Can Claim Certain Business Deductions Even if You Are Operating Illegally Under Your State Child Care Licensing Law

The Broady Tax Court case says that providers operating illegally cannot claim house expenses but can claim other business expenses such as advertising, car expenses, office supplies, repairs and maintenance, supplies, and food.

You Can Set Up a Health Reimbursement Account (HRA) by Hiring Your Spouse and Deducting Family Medical Expenses as a Business Deduction

The Speltz Tax Court case clearly allows a family child care provider to set up a medical reimbursement plan. In this case the provider did not pay her husband, but instead offered the HRA as compensation for his work. The key issue to setting up an HRA is to follow the rules to set up the spouse as a bona fide employee.

IRS Authorities

IRS Documents

- Child Care Provider Audit Technique Guide: www.irs.gov/pub/irs-utl/child_care _provider.pdf

- IRS Revenue Ruling 92-3 (1992-1 C.B. 131, 1992-3 I.R.B. 1): www.tomcopelandblog .com/irs-revenue-ruling-92-3

- IRS **Publication 587 Business Use of Home**: www.irs.gov/pub/irs-pdf/p587.pdf

- Instructions to IRS **Form 8829 Business Use of Your Home**: www.irs.gov/pub/irs -pdf/i8829.pdf

- Letter from the Acting Assistant Chief Counsel of the IRS to Minnesota Senator Rudy Boschwitz, February 6, 1990: http://tinyurl.com/y9voxyus

IRS Tax Court Cases

- *Jonelle Broady vs. Commissioner* (Tax Court Summary Opinion 2008-63, Illinois): http://tinyurl.com/yc8x44fg

- *Hewett vs. Commissioner* (Tax Court Memo 1996-110): http://tinyurl.com/o9vw4zk

- *Lauren Miller vs. Commissioner* (Tax Court Summary Opinion 2014-74): http://tinyurl .com/lfccsms

- *Robert and Dorothy Neilson vs. Commissioner* (Tax Court Decision 94-1, 1990): http:// tinyurl.com/ychbuk6r

- *Jeffrey and Simone Rayden vs. Commissioner* (Tax Court Memo 2011-1): http://tinyurl .tdgfo9th

- *Scott and Patricia Simpson vs. Commissioner* (Tax Court Memo 1997-223, May 12, 1997): http://tinyurl.com/y8pf7env

- *Peter and Maureen Speltz vs. Commissioner* (Tax Court Summary Opinion 2006-25): http://tinyurl.com/y7bm72y9

- *Brian and Pamela Uphus and Roger and Lois Walker vs. IRS Commissioner* (T.C. Memo. 1994-71): www.tomcopelandblog.com/brian-and-pamela-uphus-and-roger-and -lois-walker-vs-irs-commissioner

When to Look for Another Tax Professional

When you have disagreements with your tax professional, do everything you can to work them out. Take the time to ask questions and listen closely to the explanations. Look for a written authority and consult outside help if necessary. If you feel strongly that your position is correct or you just aren't comfortable with your tax professional, eventually you may want to consider switching to a different tax professional.

There are many family child care tax issues that are subject to legitimate differences of opinion. I do not suggest that you switch tax professionals over minor disputes. When it comes to major issues—for example, if you feel that your tax professional isn't assertive enough, or is too assertive for your comfort—don't be afraid to move on. You may want to do your own tax return (using the *Tax Workbook and Organizer* as a guide) for a while, or you can begin gathering referrals and then conduct interviews for a new tax professional.

Part 2: The Tax Organizer

Using the Tax Organizer

This Tax Organizer is designed to help you and your tax professional work together to prepare a complete and accurate tax return for your family child care business:

- This organizer will save you time and stress by listing all the information you'll need to give your tax professional and by describing the best ways to gather and calculate it.

- It will improve communication with your tax professional by giving you an organized way to provide detailed information about your business.

- It will help you take advantage of all the deductions you are entitled to by alerting your tax professional to the unique tax issues that apply to your business, including the most common errors and omissions on family child care tax returns.

- It will help you make sure that your tax return is complete and accurate by providing comprehensive review checklists for the critical forms in your business tax return (**Form 8829**, **Form 4562**, and **Schedule C**).

When filling out this organizer, you will proceed in sequence through sections on **Form 8829**, **Form 4562**, and **Schedule C**. This order will minimize the amount of backtracking that you will need to do while filling in your information. The line numbers in this organizer are based on the IRS tax forms for the 2018 tax year. Although some of the issues raised in this organizer may be helpful in double-checking your previous returns, you should use this organizer only for tax year 2018.

Before you give the completed organizer to your tax professional, be sure to make a copy for your own records. After your tax return is complete, use the review checklists for each form to double-check your return before your tax professional submits it to the IRS.

Note: Although each state has its own laws, most state tax forms are based on the numbers you report on your federal tax return. If you have any questions about the information needed to complete your state tax forms, discuss them with your tax professional.

What If You Don't Have All Your Receipts?

The organizer in this book isn't a substitute for keeping your business receipts and records. If you are audited, your entries in the Tax Organizer will be very helpful in explaining the numbers on your tax forms; however, to defend your return, you will still need to show the auditor receipts or other records to support the numbers you have recorded here.

Ideally, you will have receipts or other records to back up all the numbers that you enter in the Tax Organizer. Redleaf Press's record-keeping tools (the *Redleaf Calendar-Keeper,* the *Inventory-Keeper,* and the *Mileage-Keeper*) are specifically designed to help you record and compile the information you'll need for your tax returns. You can also use other kinds of records, such as canceled checks, credit card statements, calendar notations, pages in a ledger, electronic spreadsheets, photographs, attendance records, mileage logs, and so on.

If you don't have the proper records to support a claim, enter the item in the organizer anyway (even without a receipt) and then discuss it with your tax professional. Depending on the records that are missing, he may be able to show you how to reconstruct your records so that they will be acceptable to the IRS. (The *Family Child Care Record-Keeping Guide* also includes an explanation of how to reconstruct missing records.) Or he may advise you not to try to claim that particular expense without proper documentation.

Gathering Information for the Organizer

Each section of this organizer includes detailed instructions for gathering the appropriate information from record-keeping tools and entering it in the organizer.

- The *Redleaf Calendar-Keeper* is a monthly system for tracking your income and expenses by hand; it includes monthly and year-end charts and specialized worksheets that will make it easy to fill out this organizer.

- The *Inventory-Keeper* is a tool for tracking depreciable property, such as furniture, appliances, and equipment.

- The *Mileage-Keeper* is a tool for tracking your vehicle expenses.

If you used these record-keeping tools to track your records during the year, gathering the information you need and recording it in this organizer will be easier—you can simply print out a computer report or find a summary page and look up the totals. You will be able to skip most of the calculations in the organizer worksheets and just write the totals in at the bottom of the tables.

If you didn't use any record-keeping tools this year, you will need to collect all the records that you have kept this year, add them up, and enter the information in the worksheets in each section of the organizer.

Contact Information

Taxpayer Information

Your Name

Name of Your Business (if any)

Date You Began Your Business

Address

Phone   Cell Phone

Email

Tax Professional Information

Name of Your Tax Professional

Address

Phone   Cell Phone

Email

New IRS Simplified Method

In 2013 there was a significant change in how providers can claim their house expenses. The purpose behind the change is to make it easier for home-based businesses to claim house expenses. You can continue to fill out **Form 8829** as described below. Or, under the new rule, you might be able to claim up to $1,500 of your house expenses without any receipts directly on **Schedule C**. See the instructions to **Schedule C** for directions on how to claim your house expenses on this form.

If you use the new rule, you will not be able to deduct house depreciation, utilities, property tax, mortgage interest, house insurance, or house repairs. You will be able to claim 100% of your property tax and mortgage interest on **Schedule A**.

Using the new rule does not affect your ability to claim all other business expenses (food, toys, supplies, car expenses, etc.) on **Schedule C**.

The new Simplified Method is voluntary. You can switch back and forth between using this new rule and the old method (**Form 8829**) from one year to the next. However, if you choose the new rule for 2018 and later realize you would have been better off using **Form 8829**, you may not amend your tax return and change over to claiming house expenses on **Form 8829**.

Which Method Should You Use?

Under the new rule, home-based businesses can multiply their business square footage (300 square feet maximum) by $5 for a maximum deduction of $1,500. However, providers must first multiply $5 by their Time percentage. So, if a provider has a Time percentage of 40%, her number is now $2 ($5 x 40% = $2). She would multiply $2 by a maximum of 300 square feet for a total house deduction of $600.

The Time percentage (see page 20) is determined by dividing the number of hours you use your home for your business by the total number of hours in the year (8,750). A typical Time percentage is probably between 35% and 45%. Therefore, usually providers would be able to claim between $525 and $675 in house expenses using this new rule ($5 x 35% x 300 square feet = $525).

The small amount of house expenses that can be claimed under this new rule means that the vast majority of providers will not benefit by using this rule. If you were in business in 2017, compare the number on your **Form 8829**, line 35 to the amount you could claim under the new rule. A provider who has Time-Space percentage of 40% would have to have house expenses below $1,500 for her to benefit under the new rule ($1,500 x 40% = $600 vs. $5 x 40% x 300 square feet = $600).

Some tax preparers may be tempted to advise you to use the new rule because it will be less work for them. Because this new rule will benefit so few providers, it is extremely important to make sure you do not let your tax preparer talk you into using it, unless you understand that it will benefit you financially.

Form 8829 Expenses for Business Use of Your Home

Your tax professional will use **Form 8829** to claim the expenses—typically hundreds or even thousands of dollars—that are associated with operating a family child care business in your home.

You must file **Form 8829** unless you are providing child care in a building other than your home or you have formed a partnership or corporation. You can still use this form if you are incorporated as a single-person limited liability company (LLC).

The most important part of **Form 8829** is Part I, which shows your Time-Space percentage. In this section of the organizer, you will provide the information about your home and your business hours that your tax professional will use to calculate this critical percentage. Be sure to enter this information carefully; the numbers you enter here will have a significant impact on the amount of taxes you will owe this year.

In Part II of **Form 8829**, your tax professional will figure your allowable deduction for home business expenses. In this section of the organizer, you will provide the information for those calculations. There are two columns in this section, and to ensure that this form is completed correctly, you must list each expense in the correct column, as described in the instructions that follow.

Part III of **Form 8829** is where your tax professional will enter your home depreciation. In this section of the organizer, you will provide information about your home for that calculation. All family child care providers should take advantage of this deduction.

The amount of home business expenses that you can claim is limited by your profit or loss in this tax year. If you have more home business expenses than you can claim this year, your tax professional will use Part IV of **Form 8829** to carry over the remaining amount to the next tax year. (You don't need to provide any additional information for Part IV.)

Part I: Your Time-Space Percentage

On lines 1–7 of **Form 8829**, your tax professional will enter your Time-Space percentage. In this section of the Tax Organizer, you will provide the information needed to calculate that number, including your working hours and how you used the rooms in your home in your business.

Step 1: Gather the Information

If you used record-keeping tools to track the information needed for this section of the organizer, then (1) make sure that your records are complete; (2) compile the reports or pages described below; and (3) copy the relevant numbers into this part of the Tax Organizer.

If you didn't use any record-keeping tools last year, you will need to gather the information for this section of the Tax Organizer from other records that you have kept. If you didn't use the *Redleaf Calendar-Keeper*, go to step 2.

Redleaf Calendar-Keeper

1. During the year, record your working hours either on the monthly attendance and payment log or in the daily boxes on the monthly calendar page. At the end of each month, fill in the box in the upper right-hand corner of each monthly calendar page.

2. At the end of the year, review all the monthly totals for the year to ensure they are complete and correct.

3. Add up the year-to-date total of your business hours on the December calendar page of the 2018 *Redleaf Calendar-Keeper* (page 78). Rather than filling out all the columns in worksheets 2 and 3 (pages 18–20 in this organizer), simply put your yearly total under January in worksheet 2. Save your *Redleaf Calendar-Keeper* so you can show it to your tax professional as a backup record.

STEP 2: FILL OUT THE TAX ORGANIZER

Lines 1–3: Your Space Percentage

On lines 1–3 of **Form 8829**, your tax professional will enter information about how you used your home and will calculate your Space percentage. To do that, he will need the information on worksheet 1.

WORKSHEET 1: AREA OF YOUR HOME USED FOR BUSINESS

In column 1 below, list all the rooms in your home, including your basement and garage. In column 2, enter the total area of each room in square feet. Next, enter that area again in one of the three remaining columns (3, 4, or 5), based on how often the room is used in your business. (You can also enter part of a room in one column and another part in a different column.) Total each column in the bottom row. For more information, see the note below the worksheet.

Column 1 Room	Column 2 Square Feet	Column 3 Square Feet Used 100% for Business	Column 4 Square Feet Used Regularly for Business	Column 5 Square Feet Not Used Regularly for Business
_____	_____	_____	_____	_____
_____	_____	_____	_____	_____
_____	_____	_____	_____	_____
_____	_____	_____	_____	_____
_____	_____	_____	_____	_____
_____	_____	_____	_____	_____
_____	_____	_____	_____	_____
_____	_____	_____	_____	_____
_____	_____	_____	_____	_____
_____	_____	_____	_____	_____
Total Square Feet	_____	_____	_____	_____
	(A)	**(B)**	**(C)**	

Note: A room can be considered regularly used for business if it is used on a consistent basis, say at least two or three times a week. The children in your care don't have to be in the room while it is being used for business. In fact, you can count a room even if your licensing rules or local regulations prohibit the children from entering that part of your home.

Calculate Your Space Percentage

If you don't have an exclusive business-use room (a room used 100% for business), total B above will be zero. If this is the case, calculate your Space percentage by dividing total C by total A:

Total square feet used regularly for business	_____	**(C)**
Total square feet in your home	÷ _____	**(A)**
Your Space percentage	= _____	**(1)**

if you don't have an exclusive business-use room

      If you have an exclusive business-use room, the above Space percentage calculation does not apply to you; instead, use worksheet 4 (page 20). For a more comprehensive discussion of how to calculate your Space percentage, see the *Record-Keeping Guide.*

      It's common for family child care providers to have a Space percentage of 100%, indicating that they use all the rooms in their home on a regular basis in their business. Most providers have a Space percentage of at least 75%.

Comments

- If any of the rooms or areas in your home are used 100% for business, you will have a total for column **B**. If this is the case, be sure to use method 2 shown in worksheet 4 (see page 21) to calculate your Time-Space percentage.

- Is total **C** less than total **A**? If so, it means that you didn't use all the rooms in your home for business on a regular basis. Is this true? You should claim all the rooms that you use regularly for business purposes, including bedrooms in which the children take their naps and other rooms and areas that the children never enter.

- Did you remember to list your garage, basement, storage room, laundry room, and office in column 1? If you use any of those areas on a regular basis in your business, be sure to count them in the correct column. This will increase your Space percentage.

- You may have a basement that is one open room, a portion of which is used regularly (laundry and furnace area), while another portion is used exclusively (play area). In this case, draw an imaginary line around the play area and count it as an exclusive-use room, and count the rest of the space as a regular-use room.

Lines 4–6: Your Time Percentage

On lines 4–6 of **Form 8829**, your tax professional will enter information about your working hours and calculate your Time percentage. To do that, he will need the information on worksheets 2 and 3 (page 19).

      On these worksheets, you will add up all the hours that the children in child care were in your home, as well as all the hours that you spent in your home for business activities when the children were not present. You cannot count any time that you spent away from your home, even if it was for a business activity.

You need to have written records documenting the hours that you worked in your home. For more information about how to track those hours, see the *Record-Keeping Guide.*

WORKSHEET 2: HOURS CHILDREN WERE IN YOUR HOME

For the worksheet below, consult your attendance records and add up the number of hours that you worked each month. Count the hours each day from the time the first child arrived until the last child left. Include any hours that any of the children arrived early or stayed late, as well as any hours that you cared for children on the weekend. Do not count the hours for days that your business was closed because of illnesses, vacations, holidays, or other reasons.

January	_____	May	_____	September	_____
February	_____	June	_____	October	_____
March	_____	July	_____	November	_____
April	_____	August	_____	December	_____

Total hours children were in your home   _____ **(D)**

WORKSHEET 3: BUSINESS HOURS AT HOME WHEN CHILDREN WERE NOT PRESENT

If throughout the year you have been tracking your work hours by activity, enter the totals for the year in column 4 in the worksheet below. If you tracked your hours by month rather than by activity, simply enter your total hours for the year under column 2 next to Other, and put "1" in the next column to get your correct yearly total (**E**). If you haven't been tracking your hours, you will need to do so carefully for several months and then enter the average hours you worked each week under column 2. Multiply those averages by the number of weeks worked in the year, and then enter the results under column 4. Add up the hours in column 4.

On this worksheet you may not count any hours for these activities while the children were in your home; you already counted those hours in worksheet 2. Also, you may not count any working hours for activities away from your home (such as shopping or attending a training seminar).

Column 1 Activity	Column 2 Hours Worked per Week		Column 3 Weeks in Business		Column 4 Hours Worked in the Year
Business phone calls	_____	×	_____	=	_____
Cleaning/laundry	_____	×	_____	=	+ _____
Email/Internet activity	_____	×	_____	=	+ _____
Family child care association activities	_____	×	_____	=	+ _____
Food Program paperwork	_____	×	_____	=	+ _____
Meal preparation	_____	×	_____	=	+ _____
Parent interviews	_____	×	_____	=	+ _____
Planning/preparing activities	_____	×	_____	=	+ _____
Record keeping	_____	×	_____	=	+ _____
Other (identify: _____)	_____	×	_____	=	+ _____
Other (identify: _____)	_____	×	_____	=	+ _____

Other (identify: _____)   _____ × _____ = + _____

Other (identify: _____)   _____ × _____ = + _____

Total business hours at home when children were not present   = _____ **(E)**

Calculate Your Time Percentage

Total hours children were in your home   _____ **(D)**

Total business hours at home when children were not present   + _____ **(E)**

Total business hours for 2018   = _____ **(F)**

Total hours in the year* (enter 8,760 or part-year total)   ÷ _____ **(G)**

Your Time percentage   = _____ **(2)**

* If you were in business all year, use 8,760 on line G to calculate your Time percentage. If you started your business after January 1 or closed it before December 31, then enter the total hours for the part of the year that you were in business. When filling out **Form 8829**, cross out 8,760 on line 5, and enter your correct number. **Note to tax professional**: you will need to override your tax software to do this.

Comments

- Most family child care providers have a Time percentage between 35% and 45%. If your Time percentage is less than 35%, check your assumptions to make sure that you haven't undercounted your hours. Be sure to include all the hours that you spent on business activities when the children were not present.

- Have you included all the hours you spent on business activities in your home, such as the time you spent cleaning, preparing activities and meals, keeping your business records, and so on?

- If you worked an average of 11 hours a day, 5 days a week, for 50 weeks, your Time percentage would be 31%. You would have a Time percentage below 25% only if you worked less than the equivalent of 8 hours a day, 5 days a week.

Line 7: Your Time-Space Percentage

On line 7 of **Form 8829**, your tax professional will enter your Time-Space percentage. You will calculate that number using one of the methods shown on worksheet 4. If you have an exclusive-use room in your home, make sure that your tax professional uses the second method to calculate this number, since this will significantly increase your deductions (and lower your taxes).

WORKSHEET 4: YOUR TIME-SPACE PERCENTAGE

There are two ways to calculate your Time-Space percentage. Which one you use depends on whether you have any exclusive business-use areas in your home.

Method 1: If you don't have any exclusive-use rooms in your home, calculate your Time-Space percentage by multiplying your Space percentage (see page 18) by your Time percentage (see above):

Your Space percentage   _____ **(1)**

Your Time percentage   ×   _____ **(2)**

Your Time-Space percentage of regularly used area   =   _____ **(3)**
if you don't have an exclusive business-use room

Method 2: If you have an exclusive-use room, you are entitled to use a special rule to calculate your Time-Space percentage, and this method will give you much higher deductions. If this is the case, calculate your Time-Space percentage as follows:

Total square feet used 100% for business   _____ **(B)**

Total square feet in your home   ÷   _____ **(A)**

Space percentage of exclusive-use area   =   _____ **(4)**

Total square feet used regularly for business   _____ **(C)**

Total square feet in your home   ÷   _____ **(A)**

Space percentage of regularly used area   =   _____ **(1)**

Your Time percentage   ×   _____ **(2)**

Your Time-Space percentage of regularly used area   =   _____ **(3)**

Your Space percentage of exclusive-use area   +   _____ **(4)**

Your total Time-Space percentage   =   _____
if you have an exclusive business-use room

Note: For more information about the exclusive-room rule, see the instructions to **Form 8829** or the *Record-Keeping Guide*.

Note to tax professional: If you are using tax software and if the provider has an exclusive-use room, you will need to override the tax software, enter the Time-Space percentage on line 7, and leave lines 1–6 blank. Attach a statement to **Form 8829** showing the calculations from worksheet 4. See the instructions to **Form 8829** for further details.

Part II: Your Home Expenses

On lines 8–35 of **Form 8829**, your tax professional will figure your allowable deduction for home business expenses. To help with that, you will provide information about your home expenses during the last year in this section of the Tax Organizer.

STEP 1: GATHER THE INFORMATION

If you used record-keeping tools to track the information needed for this section of the organizer, then (1) make sure that your records are complete; (2) compile the reports or pages described below; and (3) copy the relevant numbers into this part of the organizer.

If you didn't use any record-keeping tools last year, you will need to gather the information for this section of the organizer from other records that you have kept. If you didn't use the *Redleaf Calendar-Keeper*, go to step 2.

REDLEAF CALENDAR-KEEPER

1. Make a copy of the house expenses worksheet on page 84.
2. Enter the appropriate numbers from that worksheet into column (b) in this section of the organizer.

Note: Don't apply your Time-Space percentage to these expenses before you enter them in this organizer.

STEP 2: FILL OUT THE TAX ORGANIZER

There are two columns for lines 9–21 of **Form 8829**, and you must enter your expenses in the correct column. If an expense is used 100% for your business (direct), enter it in column (a). If an expense is used both for business and personal purposes (indrect), enter it in column (b). All or most of your entries are likely to be in column (b), since family child care providers have few expenses that are exclusively for business. (Expenses that are exclusively for business include repairs to a room used only for business and the cost of fixing an item that was damaged by the children in your care.)

Your tax professional will apply your Time-Space percentage to the totals in column (b), so don't do that before you enter them below.

If you weren't in business for the entire year, enter only the expenses for the period that you were in business.

Line 9: Casualty Losses

Enter in column (a) below 100% of any casualty losses to your business property (losses caused by fire, hurricanes, earthquakes, and so on) that were not covered by insurance.

(a) _____ **(b)** _____

Line 10: Mortgage Interest Paid

Enter in column (b) below 100% of the mortgage interest that you paid for last year. Your tax professional will claim the Time-Space percentage of your mortgage interest as a business expense on line 13 of **Form 8829**. (If you itemize, you can claim the remaining personal amount of this expense on **Schedule A**.)

(a) _____ **(b)** _____

Line 11: Real Estate Taxes Paid

Enter in column (b) below 100% of the property taxes that you paid for last year. Your tax professional will claim the Time-Space percentage of your property taxes as a business expense on line 13 of **Form 8829**. (If you itemize, you can claim the remaining personal amount of this expense on **Schedule A**.)

(a) _____ **(b)** _____

Line 17: Insurance

Enter in column (b) below 100% of any homeowners or renters insurance that you paid for last year. If you purchased a business rider to your homeowners insurance to cover your business property, enter the amount you paid for this rider in column (a).

(a) _____ **(b)** _____

Line 18: Rent

If you rent your home, enter in column (b) below 100% of the rent paid last year.

(a) _____ (b) _____

Line 19: Repairs and Maintenance

Enter in column (b) below 100% of the cost of any repairs to your home, such as painting, wallpapering, fixing a leak, and so on; however, if you have any repairs to an exclusive business-use room, enter those in column (a).

(a) _____ (b) _____

Note: There has been a major new IRS regulation (Treasury Regulation Section 1.263(a)) that expands the definition of a repair versus a home improvement. Repairs can be deducted in one year. Home improvements, such as a deck or home addition, must be depreciated over 39 years.

Line 20: Utilities

Use the worksheet below to enter your total payments for utilities last year. Enter the total in column (b) below.

Gas	_____
Oil	+ _____
Electricity	+ _____
Water	+ _____
Sewer	+ _____
Garbage	+ _____
Wood/kerosene/propane	+ _____
Cable/satellite TV	+ _____
Phone services*	+ _____
Other utilities (describe)	+ _____
Total utilities paid (enter this total in column (b) below)	= _____

(a) _____ (b) _____

* On this line, include your payments for phone services such as caller ID, call waiting, answering service, and voice mail. You may also deduct your cell phone payments (as long as you have another phone line into your home). Do not count the cost of the first phone line into your home.

Note: Some providers facing rising heating bills may decide to calculate an actual business-use percentage because they believe they are using gas and electricity at a much higher rate than their Time-Space percentage indicates. If you choose to do this, enter your calculations in column (a) above, and be sure to keep careful records so you can fully support your calculations if you are audited.

Line 21: Other Expenses

Enter in column (b) below 100% of any rent or homeowner association dues for your home. If you had any other home expenses last year and aren't sure where to put them, list them below and enter the total in column (b) below:

Rent   _____

Homeowner association dues   + _____

Other home expenses (describe)   + _____

Total other home expenses   = _____

(a) _____ (b) _____

Line 29: Depreciation of Your Home

This is where your home depreciation deduction is entered from line 41 (see page 26).

Part III: Your Home Depreciation

On lines 36–41 of **Form 8829**, your tax professional will determine your allowable home depreciation. To help with that, you will provide information about the value of your home and land in this section of the Tax Organizer.

If you own your home, you will always benefit by claiming home depreciation, even if you're planning to sell your home in the near future. For more information about calculating and claiming your home depreciation, see the 2018 *Tax Workbook and Organizer*.

STEP 1: GATHER THE INFORMATION

If you used record-keeping tools to track the information needed for this section of the organizer, then (1) make sure that your records are complete; (2) compile the reports or pages described below; and (3) copy the relevant numbers into this part of the organizer.

If you didn't use any record-keeping tools last year, you will need to gather the information for this section of the organizer from other records that you have kept. If you didn't use the *Inventory-Keeper*, go to step 2.

INVENTORY-KEEPER

1. Make a copy of page 53.
2. Enter the appropriate numbers from that page in this section of the organizer.

STEP 2: FILL OUT THE TAX ORGANIZER

Line 36: Adjusted Basis of Your Home

Use the worksheet below to calculate the adjusted basis of your home. If you depreciated your home in 2017, consult your prior-year records to determine the basis of your home, and enter the result on line 38.

WORKSHEET 5: ADJUSTED BASIS OF YOUR HOME

List below all home improvements that you completed before your business began:

Column 1 Description of Improvement	Column 2 Month/Year Completed	Column 3 Cost of Improvement
_____	_____	_____
_____	_____	_____
_____	_____	_____
_____	_____	_____
_____	_____	_____

Total improvements before your business began   _____ **(I)**

Now provide the following information about the value of your home:

Original purchase price of your home   _____ **(J)**

Total improvements before your business began   +   _____ **(I)**

Adjusted basis of your home **(J + I)**   =   _____ **(K)**

Current value of your home   _____ **(L)**

Compare amounts **K** and **L**, and enter the lower of these two numbers on line 36.

Although the instructions for filling out lines 36–39 follow the directions on **Form 8829**, there is another way to calculate the basis of your home. Instead of estimating the value of the land at the time of the purchase of the home, you could compare the value of your home today without counting any home improvements. Add the home improvements to **Form 8829**, line 39.

Line 37: Value of Land

Enter the value of the land at the time you purchased your home. If you don't know what the value of your land was at that time, show your tax professional the closing papers for your home or your current property tax statement. Your tax professional will divide the value of your land today by the assessed value of your home today and multiply this percentage by the purchase price of your home to determine the estimated value of your land when it was purchased.

Value of land   _____

Line 38: Basis of Building

Enter the total of line 36 (the adjusted basis of your home) minus line 37 (the value of your land):

Adjusted basis of your home (line 36)   _____ **(K or L)**

Value of your land (line 37)   –   _____

Basis of building   =   _____

Line 39: Business Basis of Building

Enter the total of line 38 (the basis of your building) multiplied by line 7 (your Time-Space percentage). This number represents the business portion of your home.

Note: If your Time-Space percentage has changed since last tax season, be sure to adjust line 39 based on the new Time-Space percentage that you calculated on line 7 for this tax season.

Business basis of building   _____

Line 40: Depreciation Percentage

You must depreciate your home over 39 years. If you started using your home for business before this tax season, write in 2.564% on this line.

If this is the first year that you have used your home in this business, use the percentage shown below for the month when you began using your home for this business:

January	2.461%	July	1.177%
February	2.247%	August	0.963%
March	2.033%	September	0.749%
April	1.819%	October	0.535%
May	1.605%	November	0.321%
June	1.391%	December	0.107%

Depreciation percentage   _____

Line 41: Depreciation Allowable

Enter the total of line 39 multiplied by line 40. Your tax professional will also enter this number on line 29 and on line 41.

Total home depreciation   _____

Note: If your business did not make a profit last year, you will not be allowed to deduct your home depreciation. If this is the case, your tax professional will carry the amount on line 41 forward to next tax season by entering it on line 43.

Review Checklist for Form 8829

After your tax professional has completed all the forms for your tax return, you should review them before they are submitted to the IRS. Compare the numbers on your **Form 8829** to this section of the organizer and ask your tax professional to explain any discrepancies. In reviewing this form, pay particular attention to the following issues:

PART I

❑ Check that total **C** is entered on line 1, total **A** is entered on line 2, and your Space percentage is entered on line 3.

❑ Is line 1 less than line 2? If so, it means that you didn't use all the rooms in your home on a regular basis for your business. Is this true? Remember that you can claim all the rooms that you use regularly for business purposes, including bedrooms that are used for naps, garages, and other rooms that the children never enter (such as your storage room, laundry room, or office).

❐ Check that total **F** is entered on line 4. Note that the instructions for this line— "Multiply days used for daycare during year by hours used per day"—can be very misleading. What the IRS wants to know here is the number of hours that you worked in your home during the year, as calculated on worksheets 2 and 3.

❐ On line 5, if you were in business for the entire year, your tax professional should use the default total of 8,760 hours to calculate your Time percentage. If you weren't in business for the entire year, total **G** should be entered on that line instead.

❐ On line 6, check your Time percentage and carefully review the assumptions and calculations you used to get that number. This is one of the most important numbers on all your tax forms.

❐ If you used method 2 (exclusive-use room) in worksheet 4 to calculate your Time-Space percentage (**Form 8829**, line 7), your tax professional should attach a statement to **Form 8829** showing these calculations. Lines 1–6 should be left blank. (If your tax professional is using tax software, he can override Part I, enter a total on **Form 8829**, line 7, and leave lines 1–6 blank.)

❐ On **Form 8829**, line 8, your tax professional should enter the amount from **Schedule C**, line 29. This number is called your tentative profit, since it is your profit before home expenses. Your deduction for home business expenses on **Form 8829** cannot exceed this amount. If your home business expenses exceed this amount, you will have to carry forward some of those expenses to the next tax year.

PART II

❐ Check that only 100% business expenses are entered in column (a). Since these kinds of expenses are rare, almost all your expenses should be entered in column (b).

❐ Check if any of your business expenses are claimed twice, on both **Form 8829** and **Schedule C**. This is most likely to happen with expenses for insurance, repairs, and utilities, since these categories appear on both forms.

❐ Report your business liability insurance and repair of furniture, appliances, and equipment used for your business on **Schedule C**.

❐ Report your homeowners insurance and home repairs (for example, fixing the roof, repairing a broken window, interior or exterior painting) on **Form 8829**.

❐ Check that the business portion (Time-Space percentage) of your mortgage interest and real estate taxes are entered on **Form 8829**, line 13.

❐ Check that you didn't claim 100% of your property tax and mortgage interest on **Schedule A** after claiming the business portion of these items on **Form 8829**. To do this correctly, subtract the amounts claimed on **Form 8829** from the total expense of your property tax and mortgage interest before reporting them on **Schedule A**.

❐ If you own your home, check **Form 8829**, line 29, to make sure that your home depreciation deduction is shown there. If it isn't, check if you were unable to take this deduction because of a loss on **Schedule C**. If you were entitled to claim this deduction, ask your tax professional to add it; always claim your home depreciation deduction!

❏ If you weren't able to claim all your home depreciation in a previous tax year, look at line 42 on your 2017 **Form 8829**. Then check **Form 8829**, line 30, to see if this expense was carried over to this year. In addition, look at line 23 on your 2016 **Form 8829** to see if there were any other unclaimed house expenses. If so, they should appear on **Form 8829**, line 24. Bear in mind that you can only take these deductions if they don't create or add to a loss on **Schedule C**.

❏ On **Form 8829**, line 34, your tax professional should subtract the expenses that you enter on **Form 8829**, line 9, and carry them forward to **Form 4684**. From there he should enter them on **Form 4797**, and then deduct them on **Form 1040**.

❏ **Form 8829**, line 35, shows the total amount of business deductions that you are entitled to claim on **Form 8829**. Check that this amount has also been entered on **Schedule C**, line 30.

❏ If you provide child care in a building that isn't your home, you can't file **Form 8829**. If this is the case, check that your tax professional has claimed your building expenses (such as property tax, mortgage interest, homeowners insurance, home rent, utilities, home repairs, and home depreciation) on **Schedule C**.

Form 4562 Depreciation and Amortization

In December 2017, Congress passed the Tax Cuts and Jobs Act, which made major changes in the tax rules for 2018. These changes eliminated the need to use **Form 4562 Depreciation and Amortization**, with a few exceptions. The exceptions are the purchase of a home, a home improvement, and home addition.

There have been other changes in recent years, so let's clarify things with a review of these rules by discussing expenses under $2,500, expenses over $2,500, and home improvements.

Expenses under $2,500

In 2015 the IRS made a sweeping change in how to deduct items costing more than $2,500. Under the old rules, items costing more than $100 and lasting longer than one year had to be depreciated on **Form 4562**. Such items included computers, furniture, appliances, play equipment, fences, and home improvements. Now, items costing $200 or less can be deducted in one year.

Under the new rule, any item costing more than $200 and $2,500 or less can now be deducted in one year, rather than being depreciated. You can show that you are electing this rule by including the following statement with your tax return:

"Section 1.263(a)-1(f) De Minimis Safe Harbor Election

Your Name:

Address:

EIN or Social Security Number:

For the year ending December 31, 2018, I am electing the de minimis safe harbor rule under Treas. Reg. Section 1.263(a)-1(f) for items purchased for my business expenses of less than $2,500."

For more details about this rule, see my article: http://tinyurl.com/ju5ob5d.

Expenses over $2,500

The Tax Cuts and Jobs Act allows providers to deduct in one year the business portion of all expenses except for a home, a home improvement, or home addition. Computers and other office equipment must be used more than 50% of the time to use this rule. Effectively, this amends the old 50% bonus depreciation rule to a 100% bonus depreciation rule.

In other words, if you purchased a $10,000 fence and your Time-Space percentage is 40%, you can deduct $4,000 on your 2018 tax return, with no depreciation necessary. Claim these expenses directly onto **Schedule C** under "Other Expenses." Call them Equipment, or Household Items, or Fence. There is no rule about what to call an expense. **This is one of the most important tax changes for family child care providers in decades!** No longer will you have to depreciate your furniture, appliances, fences, playground equipment, patio, or driveway. If you go out of business in the next few years, there is no recapture of these deductions. In other words, you won't ever have to pay back these deductions. You can still choose to depreciate such items if you want to. A situation where you may want to depreciate items would be if you show a loss this year and want to claim higher deductions in later years.

Home Improvements

Home improvements are a complicated topic, one that has seen many changes recently. As explained on page 23, there is an expanded definition of what constitutes a repair (which is deductible in one year regardless of the cost) versus a home improvement (which is depreciated over 39 years).

For many years the general rule was that home improvements must be depreciated over 39 years on **Form 8829 Expenses for Business Use of Your Home**. As described above, there was a short-term change in 2017. If you purchased a home improvement after September 27, 2017, and before December 31, 2017, you could treat it as a repair and deduct the business portion in one year. Homes and home additions still have to be depreciated over 39 years. Congress could change this rule and allow home improvements to be eligible for the 100% bonus depreciation rule and deducted in one year. To find out the latest developments, check my website at www.tomcopelandblog.com.

When Congress passed the Tax Cuts and Jobs Act, they did not make home improvements eligible for the 100% bonus depreciation rule in 2018. Thus, home improvements in 2018 are to be depreciated over 39 years.

If you purchased a deck, garage, made a home improvement, or other home addition, there are two circumstances that allow those costs to be deducted in one year, even though they don't qualify for the 100% bonus rule. These are the Section 179 rule and the Safe Harbor for Small Taxpayers rule.

The Section 179 Rule

If you used your home improvement more than 50% of the time for your business, you can now use the Section 179 rule and deduct the business portion in one year for 2018. To take advantage of this rule, your Time-Space percentage should be more than 50%. If not, you should keep records to show that you did use the home improvement more than 50% of the time for your business. The best way to show that is to track the hours of business and personal use on a calendar for several months. The only drawback of using the Section 179 rule is that if you go out of business or use the item 50% or less in later years, you will have to pay back some of the deduction you claimed.

Enter your home improvements used more than 50% of the time in your business on Part I of **Form 4562**.

The Safe Harbor for Small Taxpayers Rule

The Safe Harbor for Small Taxpayers rule allows providers to deduct in one year the cost of a certain amount of home improvements made to their home. This includes a home addition, remodeling a kitchen or bathrooms, or a new furnace or a new deck. The amount that can be deducted in one year is the lesser amount of $10,000 or 2% of the unadjusted basis of your home (the purchase price of your home minus the value of the land at the time you bought it). For example, if you purchased your home for $300,000 you could deduct up to $6,000 of improvements in one year ($300,000 x 2% = $6,000, which is less than $10,000). If you purchased your home for $500,000 or more, you can deduct up to $10,000 of improvements.

To use this rule you must elect it by filing a statement with your tax return. Here's the statement you should use:

"Section 1.263(a)-3(h) Safe Harbor Election for Small Taxpayers

Your Name:

Address:

EIN or Social Security Number:

For the year ending December 31, 2018, I am electing the safe harbor election for small taxpayers under Treas. Reg. Section 1.263(a)-3(g) for the following: (list your improvements)."

For more details about this rule, see my article: http://tinyurl.com/h54ngbv.

Make sure your tax preparer has attached this, or a similar, statement to your tax return.

Part I: Your Section 179 Deductions

Other than using the Section 179 rule for qualified home improvements, most providers will not claim any other items under this rule. That's because you can deduct most every other expense in one year on **Schedule C**, without worrying about the restriction of having to use it more than 50% of the time for your business to qualify for the Section 179 rule. If you choose to use the Section 179 rule for expenses other than a home improvement, consult with your tax preparer about the consequences of doing so.

On lines 1–13 of **Form 4562**, your tax professional will enter your deductions for items that qualify for the Section 179 rule. In this section of the Tax Organizer, you will provide information about any items that you bought this year and wish to deduct under Section 179.

STEP 1: GATHER THE INFORMATION

If you used record-keeping tools to track the information needed for this section of the organizer, then (1) make sure that your records are complete; (2) compile the reports or pages described below; and (3) copy the relevant numbers into this part of the organizer.

If you didn't use any record-keeping tools last year, you will need to gather the information for this section of the organizer from other records that you have kept. If you didn't use the *Inventory-Keeper*, go to step 2.

INVENTORY-KEEPER

1. Consult the tables of depreciable items on pages 17–49 and 53–54 and make a list of all the depreciable items you purchased last year.

2. Review that list and determine if any of the items meet the requirements for the Section 179 rule (see line 6). Decide if you would like to use the Section 179 rule to deduct any of these items this year.

3. Mark the items you have selected and enter them in this section of the organizer.

STEP 2: FILL OUT THE TAX ORGANIZER

Line 6: Your Section 179 Deductions

To qualify for Section 179, an item must have been purchased this tax year and have been used more than 50% of the time in your business during this tax year. You don't want to use the Section 179 rule for nearly all items because it puts you at risk for recapture if you go out of business or use it less than 50% of the time in later years.

List below all the items you bought last year that you wish to deduct under Section 179 (you don't need to total these items). Enter the actual business-use percentage of each item under column 4. You must keep records to show how you determined this percentage.

Column 1 Description	Column 2 Cost	Column 3 Date Purchased	Column 4 Business-Use Percentage

Note: Double-check that all the items listed above were used more than 50% in your business this year.

Comments

- If you qualify to use the Section 179 rule, you may still choose to depreciate the item under the regular depreciation rules in Part III of **Form 4562**. If you wish to do that, don't list the item above; instead, list it in the next section of this organizer.

- You may not want to use Section 179 if you plan to close your child care business within the next few years or if you aren't sure that you'll continue to use the item more than 50% in your business. If either of these situations occur after you have used Section 179, you will end up having to pay back some of the deductions that you have claimed.

Part II: Special Depreciation Allowance

Line 14: This is where to enter any items costing more than $2,500 that you want to apply the 100% bonus depreciation rule. Look on pages 33-34 to see if you purchased any items (new or used) that cost more than $2,500. If so, it's to your advantage to use the 100% bonus depreciation rule and enter these items here.

Part III: Your Depreciation Deductions

On lines 17–20 of **Form 4562**, your tax professional will enter your depreciation deductions. In this section of the Tax Organizer, you will provide information about the depreciable items that you purchased this year. As a rule, you'll also be claiming a depreciation deduction for items that you purchased in previous years (line 17).

STEP 1: GATHER THE INFORMATION

If you used record-keeping tools to track the information needed for this section of the organizer, then (1) make sure that your records are complete; (2) compile the reports or pages described below; and (3) copy the relevant numbers into this part of the organizer.

If you didn't use any record-keeping tools last year, you will need to gather the information for this section of the organizer from other records that you have kept. If you didn't use the *Inventory-Keeper,* go to step 2.

INVENTORY-KEEPER

1. Consult the tables of depreciable items on pages 17–49 and 53–54 and make a list of all the depreciable items that you purchased last year.
2. Cross off any items that you have decided to deduct this year under Section 179.
3. Enter the remaining items you purchased last year in this section of the organizer.

STEP 2: FILL OUT THE TAX ORGANIZER

Section A: Items Placed in Service in a Previous Tax Year

On **Form 4562**, line 17, your tax professional will enter your depreciation deduction for all the items that you started using in your business before last year and haven't fully depreciated yet. If you have already started depreciating these items, you should give your tax professional a worksheet or other record showing what items you were depreciating before last year. If you didn't claim depreciation of household items such as furniture or appliances or if you are not sure whether your depreciation deductions were entered correctly on your 2017 tax return, discuss this with your tax professional.

You aren't required to identify the items on this line by attaching a depreciation schedule; however, you may want to ask your tax professional for a copy of the depreciation schedule he uses to calculate this total so that you can double-check the items on this line against your records.

Section B: Depreciable Items First Placed in Service in 2018

In this section, your tax professional will enter depreciation deductions for the items that you began using in your business in 2018, based on the information you provide below. If there is more than one item in a category, he will enter the total on **Form 4562** and attach a depreciation schedule to identify the individual items. Remember, because of the new tax laws in 2018, most providers do not need to depreciate any items except a deck, garage, home improvement, other home addition, or vehicle. It only makes sense to depreciate other items if you want to show a larger profit in 2018.

For each line below there is a category (such as Personal Property) and a brief description of the typical items in that category (for example, "furniture and appliances"). For a comprehensive list of the items you can depreciate in each of these categories, consult the *Record-Keeping Guide*. If you claimed an item using the Section 179 rule (see page 30), do not list it again here. Under column 4, enter either your Time-Space percentage or your actual business-use percentage; if you use the latter, keep records to show how you calculated your actual business-use percentage. If you run out of lines to enter all your depreciation items, attach a separate page to the Tax Organizer listing these additional items.

Note: Some of the lines in section B are omitted below, since they don't apply to family child care businesses.

Line 19c: Personal Property

List below any furniture, appliances, play equipment, carpeting, or vinyl flooring that you purchased in 2018 and used in your business.

Column 1 Description	Column 2 Cost	Column 3 Date Purchased	Column 4 Business Use Percentage

Line 19e: Land Improvement

List below any fences, patios, new driveways, swimming pools, or other land improvements that you purchased in 2018 and used in your business.

Column 1 Description	Column 2 Cost	Column 3 Date Purchased	Column 4 Business Use Percentage

Line 19i: Home Improvement

List below any home improvements (such as remodeling or a new roof, furnace, or air-conditioning system) that you purchased in 2018 and used in your business.

Column 1 Description	Column 2 Cost	Column 3 Date Purchased	Column 4 Business Use Percentage

Part V: Listed Property

Line 26 or 27: Computers

List below any computers, printers, copiers, or fax machines that you purchased in 2018 and used in your business.

Column 1 Description	Column 2 Cost	Column 3 Date Purchased	Column 4 Business Use Percentage

Line 27: Vehicle

If you are using the actual vehicle expenses method (see page 41), you may be entitled to depreciate your vehicle. If you are not sure if you will be using the standard mileage rate method or the actual vehicle expenses method, enter your vehicle information below and discuss this with your tax professional.

Column 1 Description	Column 2 Cost	Column 3 Date Purchased	Column 4 Business Use Percentage

Review Checklist for Form 4562

After your tax professional has completed all the forms for your tax return, you should review them before they are submitted to the IRS. Compare the numbers on your **Form 4562** to this section of the organizer and ask your tax professional to explain any discrepancies.

Many tax professionals use their own worksheets to track depreciation expenses over the years. These worksheets show exactly how the depreciation deduction for each item was calculated. You should ask your tax professional for a copy of these depreciation worksheets every year and keep them with your tax records. These records will be especially helpful if you ever have to switch to another tax professional.

This section of the Tax Organizer asks that you provide information for only Parts I, II, and III of **Form 4562**; however, in reviewing this form, you should also check Parts IV and V, as described below. In reviewing this form, pay particular attention to the following issues:

PART I

❒ Ask your tax professional for a copy of the depreciation schedule that details each item you are listing in this section, and then check each item to be sure it was used more than 50% in your business this year.

PART III, SECTION A

❒ If you have been in business for more than a year, **Form 4562**, line 17, should show a depreciation deduction for items you started using in your business before this tax year. Family child care providers are almost always entitled to claim a depreciation deduction for previous years. If there isn't an amount listed on line 17, this is probably an error; be sure to discuss this with your tax professional.

❒ If you aren't sure whether the amount shown on line 17 is correct, ask your tax professional for a copy of the depreciation schedule for this line so you can see how it was calculated. Compare the list on that depreciation schedule to your records to make sure that the total on line 17 includes all the items that you are entitled to depreciate.

❒ If you began your business within the last seven years, check that line 17 includes depreciation for the furniture and appliances you purchased before you started your business. (You will need to inventory these items and estimate their value at the time your business began. If they were worth $10,000 and you have a Time-Space percentage of 40%, this deduction would be worth about $570 a year for seven years. For more information, see the *Inventory-Keeper* or the *Record-Keeping Guide*.)

❒ If you discover that you didn't claim the depreciation deductions you were entitled to in a previous tax year, you may be able to use **Form 3115 Application for Change in Accounting Method** to recapture your unclaimed depreciation. For more information, see the 2018 *Tax Workbook and Organizer*.

PART III, SECTION B

❒ Depreciation rules are complex. If you don't understand how the calculations were made for your depreciable items, ask your tax professional for an explanation. The

2018 *Tax Workbook and Organizer* explains all the depreciation rules in detail for the year. Depreciation rules can change from year to year.

PART IV

❏ If your tax professional has claimed any listed property on Part V of **Form 4562** (see page 34), check that the total on line 28 has also been entered on line 21.

❏ Line 22 shows your total depreciation deductions for the year. Check that this number has been transferred to **Schedule C**, line 13.

PART V

❏ If you used a vehicle in your business, make sure that "yes" is checked next to the boxes on **Form 4562**, lines 24a and 24b. If these boxes aren't checked, they could trigger an audit of your return.

❏ If you used a vehicle in your business last year, check that the vehicle is listed on **Form 4562**, line 26 or 27, and that lines 30–36 are filled out, even if you used the standard mileage rate method for your vehicle expenses.

❏ If you used the actual vehicle expenses method of claiming your vehicle expenses, check that your tax professional has also claimed a deduction for vehicle depreciation on **Form 4562**, line 26 or 27.

Schedule C Profit or Loss from Business

Your tax professional will use **Schedule C** to report your business income, claim your business expenses, and calculate the profit or loss from your business. (Although some small-business owners may be able to use **Schedule C-EZ** instead of **Schedule C**, no family child care provider should ever do so.)

In Part I of **Schedule C**, your tax professional will report the business income that you received from parents and government subsidies, as well as the reimbursements you received from the Food Program.

Part II of **Schedule C** is where your tax professional will enter the business expenses that you are claiming this year. This section of the Tax Organizer starts with worksheets to determine your vehicle and food expenses. These are followed by a section that lists all the business expense lines on **Schedule C**. You will enter all your business expenses here, including the vehicle and food totals that you calculated on the worksheets.

When recording your expenses for **Schedule C**, bear in mind that there are no rules about which line you must use to claim any given expense.

Part I: Your Income

On lines 1–7 of **Schedule C**, your tax professional will enter the business income that you received last year. In this section of the Tax Organizer, you will list all your business income this year, including the payments you received from child care parents, government subsidy programs, and the Food Program.

STEP 1: GATHER THE INFORMATION

If you used record-keeping tools to track the information needed for this section of the organizer, then (1) make sure that your records are complete; (2) compile the reports or pages described below; and (3) copy the relevant numbers into the organizer.

If you didn't use any record-keeping tools last year, you will need to gather the information for this section of the organizer from other records that you have kept. If you didn't use the *Redleaf Calendar-Keeper,* go to step 2.

REDLEAF CALENDAR-KEEPER

In the *Redleaf Calendar-Keeper,* you may have recorded your income either on the monthly attendance and payment log or on the payment and income record (pages 86–93).

If you used the Attendance and Payment Log:

1. Find Total Y-T-D Income under Parent Fee Income Recvd on page 81. This is your total income from parents and government subsidy programs. Enter this number as the total of **M + N** below.

2. Find Total Y-T-D Income under Food Program Income Recvd on page 81. This is your total Food Program income. Enter this number as total **O** on page 38 in this organizer.

If you used the Payment and Income Record:

1. Find the 2017 total on page 93. This is your total income from parents and government subsidy programs. Enter this number as the total of **M + N** in worksheet 6 below.

2. Find the quarterly Food Program totals on the payment and income record on pages 87, 89, 91, and 93, and add them up to get your total Food Program income. Enter this number as total **O** on page 38 in this organizer.

Note: You can't track the Food Program reimbursements for your own children in the *Redleaf Calendar-Keeper*; if you're using this tool, you will need to track these reimbursements separately.

STEP 2: FILL OUT THE TAX ORGANIZER

Line 1: Income from Parents and Subsidy Programs

WORKSHEET 6: PAYMENTS FROM PARENTS AND SUBSIDY PROGRAMS

Enter below all the payments you received from the parents of each child in your care (in column 2) and any subsidy payments you received for providing care to each family (in column 3). Report only income that you received during last year. Don't report any income that you earned last year but didn't receive until this year.

If you received a **Form 1099 Miscellaneous Income** for all or part of a parent subsidy listed in column 3, enter the amount as **Form 1099** income (in column 4).

Column 1 Name of Parent	Column 2 Total Received from This Parent	Column 3 Subsidy from County or State for This Parent	Column 4 Form 1099 Income for This Subsidy
_____	_____	_____	_____
_____	_____	_____	_____
_____	_____	_____	_____
_____	_____	_____	_____
_____	_____	_____	_____
_____	_____	_____	_____

Totals _____

                     (M)   **(N)**

Total parent and subsidy payments **(M + N)** _____

Note: Your tax professional will need to add a note to **Schedule C** stating how much of your income was listed on a **Form 1099**; for example, "**Form 1099** Income: $2,300."

Line 6: Food Program Income

Enter below all reimbursements you received from the Food Program during the last year. If you received a reimbursement in January 2018 for December 2017 meals, include it below. (Don't include any payments you received in January 2019 for December 2018 meals.)

If you received any reimbursements for your own children, subtract them from your total Food Program income, since those payments aren't taxable.

Total Food Program reimbursements _____**(O)**

Food Program reimbursements for your own children   – _____

Taxable Food Program income   = _____

Note: Some tax professionals include Food Program reimbursements on line 1 of **Schedule C** rather than entering them separately on line 6. Although both methods are correct, we recommend that your tax professional enter these reimbursements on line 6 and add a note in the margin that this is your taxable Food Program income. This will alert the IRS that you are properly reporting these payments as business income.

Part II: Your Vehicle Expenses

Your tax professional will claim your vehicle expenses on line 9 of **Schedule C**. In this section of the Tax Organizer, you will determine your deduction for vehicle expenses. Later you will transfer that amount to line 9 on page 46 of this organizer.

There are two ways to claim the business expenses for your vehicle: the standard mileage rate method and the actual vehicle expenses method. Either of these methods can also be used if you lease your vehicle. On the worksheets in this section, you can calculate your deduction using each method and determine which one gives you the higher deduction.

If you began using the vehicle in your business in 2017 or if you used the standard mileage rate method for this vehicle in 2017, you may use either the standard mileage rate method or the actual vehicle expenses method in 2018. If you used the actual vehicle expenses method for this vehicle in 2017, you must continue using this method in 2018.

STEP 1: GATHER THE INFORMATION

If you used record-keeping tools to track the information needed for this section of the organizer, then (1) make sure that your records are complete; (2) compile the reports or pages described below; and (3) copy the relevant numbers into this part of the organizer.

If you didn't use any record-keeping tools last year, you will need to gather the information for this section of the organizer from other records that you have kept.

Note: When checking that your mileage records are complete, make sure you have included business trips that you recorded only on your monthly calendar pages because you didn't spend any money on that trip—such as trips to the library or to school, field trips, or trips to other destinations. Also review other records, such as photos or bank deposit slips, for evidence of any other business trips.

If you didn't use the *Redleaf Calendar-Keeper* or the *Mileage-Keeper*, go to step 2.

REDLEAF CALENDAR-KEEPER

1. If you tracked your business miles on the monthly expense pages in the *Redleaf Calendar-Keeper*, find the year-to-date total under Miles on page 83.

2. To avoid having to reenter all your trips in worksheet 8 (page 40 in this organizer), follow these directions: Put all trips under column 1. Put your total business miles for the year under column 2. Put "1" under column 3. This will calculate your correct total as **Q** on page 40 of this organizer.

MILEAGE-KEEPER

If you used the *Mileage-Keeper* to compile your mileage and vehicle expenses, your records should be on the following pages:

1. If you used the standard mileage rate method to calculate your vehicle expenses, find your records of business mileage and other allowable business vehicle expenses on pages 34–35.

2. If you used the actual vehicle expenses method to calculate your vehicle expenses, find your records of business mileage and actual vehicle expenses on pages 44–45.

3. Enter the appropriate totals from these pages in worksheet 11.

STEP 2: FILL OUT THE TAX ORGANIZER

Worksheets for Vehicle Expenses

If you used more than one vehicle for your business last year, make a copy of this section of the organizer for each vehicle and fill out the worksheets to determine the best deduction for each vehicle. Choose the best method to claim your expenses for each vehicle and then add up those deductions to get your total vehicle expenses.

WORKSHEET 7: VEHICLE INFORMATION

Make and model of vehicle	_____
Date first used in your business	_____
Purchase price of vehicle	_____
Fair market value of vehicle when first used in business	_____
Odometer reading on December 31 of last year	_____
Odometer reading on January 1 of last year	– _____
Total miles driven last year	= _____ (P)

WORKSHEET 8: BUSINESS MILEAGE

You can count as business miles any trips for which the primary purpose was business. You should keep written records for all your business trips. You can use the *Redleaf Calendar-Keeper* or the *Mileage-Keeper*, or you can keep receipts, canceled checks, credit card statements, photographs, and so on.

List in the worksheet all the trips for which the primary purpose was business. In column 1, list the destination (grocery store, school, library, park, bank). In column 2, enter the round-trip mileage for that destination. In column 3, enter the number of business trips to that destination. In column 4, calculate your total mileage for each destination, and add up your total mileage.

If you have kept a complete mileage log for last year, you don't need to fill in this entire chart; simply enter the total business miles from your log as total **Q**.

Column 1 Destination	Column 2 Round-Trip Mileage		Column 3 Number of Business Trips		Column 4 Business Miles This Year
_____	_____	X	_____	=	_____
_____	_____	X	_____	=	_____
_____	_____	X	_____	=	_____
_____	_____	X	_____	=	_____
_____	_____	X	_____	=	_____
_____	_____	X	_____	=	_____
_____	_____	X	_____	=	_____
_____	_____	X	_____	=	_____
_____	_____	X	_____	=	_____
_____	_____	X	_____	=	_____

_____	_____	x	_____	=	_____	
_____	_____	x	_____	=	_____	

Total business miles   _____(Q)

Calculate your business-use percentage for this vehicle:

Total business miles   _____(Q)

Total miles driven last year   ÷   _____ (P)

Vehicle business-use percentage   =   _____ % (R)

WORKSHEET 9: STANDARD MILEAGE RATE METHOD

Multiply your business miles by the 2018 mileage rate.

Business miles January 1 through December 31_____   x 0.545   =   _____

Your business miles deduction   =   _____ (S)

There are certain vehicle expenses that you are entitled to claim under both methods of calculating your vehicle expenses. Calculate this amount as shown below. First enter your total payments for interest on your vehicle loan and the personal property tax on your vehicle (as shown on your license registration invoice). Add up those expenses and multiply the total by the business-use percentage for this vehicle. Finally, add your actual business expenses for parking, tolls, and ferry charges this year.

Interest on vehicle loan   _____

Personal property tax on vehicle   +   _____

Total loan interest and tax   =   _____

Vehicle business-use percentage   x   _____ % (R)

Your business portion   =   _____

Business parking, tolls, and ferry fees   +   _____

Your business expenses deduction   =   _____ (T)

Calculate your standard mileage rate deduction:

Your business mileage deduction   _____ (S)

Your business expenses deduction   +   _____ (T)

Your total standard mileage rate deduction   =   _____ (U)

WORKSHEET 10: ACTUAL VEHICLE EXPENSES METHOD

If you use this method, you can deduct all the expenses listed below, but you must keep records of all your vehicle expenses so that you can add them up at the end of the year. If you used this method for your vehicle in 2017, you are required to use it again (for that vehicle) in 2018.

Gas   _____

Oil/lube/filter   +   _____

Tune-up/tires   + _____

Repairs/maintenance   + _____

Wash/wax   + _____

Supplies   + _____

Vehicle insurance   + _____

Vehicle lease costs for last year   + _____

Other (describe):

_____   + _____

_____   + _____

_____   + _____

Total actual vehicle expenses   = _____ (V)

Note: Don't add your vehicle loan interest, personal property tax on the vehicle, or actual business expenses for parking, tolls, and ferry charges under Other expenses above. That will double-count those expenses, since you'll add them as total **T** after you apply the business-use deduction to the above expenses.

Total actual vehicle expenses   _____ (V)

Vehicle business-use percentage   x   _____ % (R)

Your business-use deduction   =   _____ (W)

Your business expenses deduction   +   _____ (T)

Your total actual vehicle expenses deduction =   _____ (X)*

* The above total does not include amounts you may be able to claim for your vehicle depreciation. If you depreciated your vehicle in 2017, discuss this with your tax professional. If this is your first year in business, fill in the following information.

Year your vehicle was purchased   _____

Purchase price of your vehicle   _____

Fair market value of your vehicle when
you first started using it in your business   _____

WORKSHEET 11: YOUR BEST DEDUCTION FOR VEHICLE EXPENSES

If you used the actual vehicle expenses method for a vehicle in 2017, you are required to use that method again (for that vehicle) in 2018. In this case, enter total **X** on line 9 on page 46 of this organizer.

If you used the standard mileage rate method for this vehicle in 2017, you can use either method. Compare your deductions and enter the higher amount **Y** on line 9 on page 46 of this organizer.

If you first used your vehicle for business last year and you chose the Actual Vehicle Expenses Method, you must continue to use this method for as long as you use your vehicle in your business.

Total standard mileage rate deduction   _____(U)

Total actual vehicle expenses deduction   _____(X)

Enter the higher of the above amounts   _____(Y)

*(your tax professional will enter this
amount on line 9 of **Schedule C**)*

Part II: Your Food Expenses

Your tax professional will claim your food expenses on one of the blank lines in Part V of **Schedule C**. In this section of the Tax Organizer, you will determine your deduction for food expenses. Later you will enter that amount on one of the blank lines under Part V of **Schedule C** (on the form in the back of this organizer).

There are two ways to calculate your food expenses—you can use the IRS standard meal allowance rate or you can deduct the actual cost of the food that you purchased. You may calculate your food expenses using either method and choose the method that gives you a higher deduction each year. For each method there are also specific requirements about the kinds of records that you must keep (see worksheets 12 and 13). For a comprehensive discussion of these two methods, see the *Record-Keeping Guide*.

Regardless of which method you use to calculate your food expenses, you can always deduct other food-related items such as kitchen supplies (paper plates, napkins, paper towels), the actual cost of the food you serve to your employees, and food that is used in an activity (dry pasta glued on paper for an art project). Deduct these items under the most appropriate expense line on **Schedule C**, such as Supplies (for kitchen supplies) or Activity Expenses in Part V (for food used in an activity).

Step 1: Gather the Information

If you used record-keeping tools to track the information needed for this section of the organizer, then (1) make sure that your records are complete; (2) compile the reports or pages described below; and (3) copy the relevant numbers into this part of the organizer.

If you didn't use any record-keeping tools last year, you will need to gather the information for this section of the organizer from other records that you have kept. If you didn't use the *Redleaf Calendar-Keeper*, go to step 2.

Note: Depending on how you entered the information about your meals or food expenses in the record-keeping tools, you may need to double-check that the information you are compiling includes only the food that was eaten by the children in your care.

Redleaf Calendar-Keeper

1. If you used the standard meal allowance rate to calculate your food expenses, find the year-end meal tally on page 95.

2. Enter this number as total **Z** in worksheet 12 on page 44.

3. If you saved all your food receipts and entered your business food expenses in the monthly expense report pages, find the yearly total of your actual food expenses on your December expense report (page 83).

4. Enter this number as total **AA** in worksheet 14 on page 45.

STEP 2: FILL OUT THE TAX ORGANIZER

WORKSHEETS FOR FOOD EXPENSES

WORKSHEET 12: THE STANDARD MEAL ALLOWANCE RATE

If you use this method, you can claim your food expenses without having to keep any food receipts; however, you must keep the following records throughout the year:

- the name of each child in your care;

- the dates and hours that each child attended your program; and

- the number of meals that you served to each child.

If you participated in the Food Program last year, save copies of your monthly Food Program claim forms. Record on these forms any meals you served that weren't reimbursed. (You can also record them elsewhere, such as in the *Redleaf Calendar-Keeper.*)

1. Add up the meals and snacks you served to the children in your care during the year, showing the totals for breakfast, lunch/dinner, and snack. Include both the meals that were reimbursed by the Food Program and the meals that weren't reimbursed by the Food Program. You may claim up to one breakfast, one lunch, one dinner, and three snacks per child per day (if you serve them).

2. Do not count any meals or snacks that you served to your own children in this total, even if you were reimbursed by the Food Program for these meals. (You can't count these meals as a business expense.)

3. Multiply the total meals and snacks that you served last year by the standard meal allowance rates for 2018: $1.31 for breakfast, $2.46 for lunch/dinner, and $0.73 for snack (these are the same rates as 2017). The rates are higher in Alaska and Hawaii. For these rates, go to https://tinyurl.com/yc2ylcnw. You can use this rate to determine your food expenses, whether you are receiving the higher (Tier I) or lower (Tier II) reimbursement rate, and even if you aren't participating in the Food Program.

Number of breakfasts _____ x $1.31 = _____

Number of lunches/dinners _____ x $2.46 = + _____

Number of snacks _____ x $0.73 = + _____

Total food expenses = _____

4. Enter the final amount as total **Z** below.

Total food expenses using the standard meal allowance rate _____ **(Z)**

If you wish, you can copy the meal form and year-end meal tally from the previous pages and use them to add up your meals and calculate your food deduction using the standard meal allowance rate.

WORKSHEET 13: THE ACTUAL COST OF FOOD METHOD

There are many ways to calculate your actual food costs. The simplest and most accurate method is to estimate an average cost per child per meal and multiply it by the number of meals and snacks served. Bear in mind that if you use this method, you must save all your business and personal food receipts to support your deduction. For more information, consult the *Record-Keeping Guide*.

If you calculate your food deduction using the actual cost of food, enter it as total **AA** below.

Total food expenses using the actual cost of food method   _____**(AA)**

WORKSHEET 14: YOUR BEST DEDUCTION FOR FOOD EXPENSES

If you have used only one method to track and calculate your food expenses, enter the total you have calculated as "Food Expenses" on one of the blank lines in Part V of **Schedule C**.

If you have calculated your food expenses using both methods and have the records to support either one, total **AB** below is your best deduction for food expenses; enter this amount as "Food Expenses" on one of the blank lines in Part V of **Schedule C**.

Total food expenses using the standard meal allowance rate   _____ **(Z)**

Total food expenses using the actual cost of food method   _____**(AA)**

Enter the higher of the above amounts   _____**(AB)**

Part II: Your Business Expenses

On lines 8–32 of **Schedule C**, your tax professional will claim your business expenses for last year. To help her do that, you will provide information about your expenses, including the deductions for vehicle and food expenses that you calculated on worksheets 11 and 14 in this section of the Tax Organizer.

STEP 1: GATHER THE INFORMATION

If you used record-keeping tools to track the information needed for this section of the organizer, then (1) make sure that your records are complete; (2) compile the reports or pages described below; and (3) copy the relevant numbers into this part of the organizer.

If you didn't use any record-keeping tools last year, you will need to gather the information for this section of the organizer from other records that you have kept. If you didn't use the *Redleaf Calendar-Keeper,* go to step 2.

REDLEAF CALENDAR-KEEPER

1. If you entered your business expenses on a consistent basis on the monthly expense pages, total these amounts on the income tax worksheet (page 85).

2. Check that you have properly identified the expenses that are 100% for business and that you have applied your Time-Space percentage to all the other items. (If you find an error, you may need to redo step 1.)

3. Enter the appropriate numbers from this report in this section of the organizer.

STEP 2: FILL OUT THE TAX ORGANIZER

When entering your **Schedule C** expenses, it's important to know whether an item is used 100% for business or shared with your family. An item that you claim as 100% for business can never be used for personal purposes (after business hours). Don't claim an item as 100% business unless it actually meets this qualification.

You can deduct items that are used for shared business and personal purposes, using your Time-Space percentage (**Form 8829**, line 7). If your actual business use of the item is much higher than your Time-Space percentage, you may calculate your actual business-use percentage for that item and use it to determine your deduction. For more information, see the *Record-Keeping Guide*.

You may not want to enter your Time-Space percentage when filling out lines 8–27 on **Schedule C**. This is because you may not be certain what it is until after discussing it with your tax preparer. What's important is that you identify for each item whether it is used 100% for your business or is used for both business and personal purposes. Items that are used only by you or your family are never deductible. These nondeductible items include your children's clothing, any toys that they don't share with the children in child care, and any parking or traffic tickets that you incur, even on a business trip.

Note: In addition to the information requested below, your tax professional will also transfer the business expenses that were calculated on **Form 8829** or **Form 4562** (such as depreciation) to the appropriate lines on **Schedule C**.

Line 8: Advertising

Enter below 100% of your business advertising expenses, such as business cards, welcome mats, newspaper ads, keepsakes, and so on. See the *Marketing Guide* for a list of over 100 deductions you can include on this line.

Deductible advertising expenses   _____

Line 9: Vehicle Expenses

Enter below your deduction for vehicle expenses from worksheet 11.

Deductible vehicle expenses   _____

Line 15: Insurance

Add up your insurance expenses for your business.

Liability insurance   _____

Workers' compensation insurance for employees   +   _____

Deductible insurance expenses   =   _____

Note: Enter 100% of your payments for business liability and workers' compensation insurance for your employees. Don't include your homeowners insurance here; your tax professional will enter it on **Form 8829**.

Line 16b: Interest

Calculate the deductible total of your interest expenses below.

Your total shared business and personal interest expenses   _____

Your Time-Space percentage   x   _____

Business portion of interest expenses   =   _____

Your 100% interest expenses   + _____

Deductible interest   = _____

Note: Your shared interest expenses include credit card interest on items used both for business and personal purposes. For your 100% interest expenses, enter the interest you paid on loans strictly for business purchases. Don't include your mortgage interest here; your tax professional will enter it on **Form 8829** (and **Schedule A**, if you itemize).

Line 17: Legal and Professional Services

Enter the amount you paid your tax professional last year for preparing the forms for your business—**Schedule C**, **Schedule SE**, **Form 4562**, and **Form 8829**. Also include any amounts you paid to a lawyer or a bookkeeper for your business.

Deductible legal and professional services   _____

Note: Ask your tax professional to list her fees for business and personal tax forms separately on her invoice. If you itemize, you can deduct the cost of preparing your personal tax forms on **Schedule A**.

Line 18: Office Expenses

Calculate the deductible total of your office expenses below.

Your total shared business and personal office expenses   _____

Your Time-Space percentage   X _____

Business portion of office expenses   = _____

Your 100% office expenses   + _____

Deductible office expenses   = _____

Note: Your 100% business expenses include any office expenses for your business (bank charges, books, magazines, desk supplies, receipt books) as well as any education or training expenses for your business.

Line 20: Rent

Calculate the deductible total of your rental expenses below.

Your total shared business and personal rental expenses   _____

Your Time-Space percentage   X _____

Business portion of rental expenses   = _____

Your 100% rental expenses   + _____

Deductible rental expenses   = _____

Note: Your 100% business expenses might include video rentals, carpet cleaning equipment, and so on. Don't include any rent you pay on your home here; that is entered on **Form 8829**.

Line 21: Repairs and Maintenance

Calculate the deductible total of your repair and maintenance expenses below.

Your total shared business and personal repair
and maintenance expenses   _____

Your Time-Space percentage   X _____

Business portion of repair and maintenance expenses   = _____

Your 100% repair and maintenance expenses   + _____

Deductible repair and maintenance expenses   = _____

Note: Your 100% business expenses would include any repairs and maintenance for your business property, such as appliance service contracts and repairs of toys or furniture. Don't include any home repairs or maintenance here; those amounts are entered on **Form 8829**.

Line 22: Supplies

Calculate the deductible total of your expenses for supplies below.

Your total shared business and personal expenses for supplies   _____

Your Time-Space percentage   X _____

Business portion of expenses for supplies   = _____

Your 100% expenses for supplies   + _____

Deductible expenses for supplies   = _____

Note: Your expenses for supplies might include children's supplies (craft items and games), kitchen supplies (plastic wrap, garbage bags, and food containers), and outdoor supplies (weed killer, gas and oil for your lawn mower, and so on).

Line 23: Taxes and Licenses

Calculate the deductible total of your taxes and license expenses below.

License fees   _____

Employer payroll taxes*   + _____

Business personal property taxes   + _____

Other business taxes and licenses   + _____

Deductible taxes and license expenses   = _____

* Payroll taxes include Social Security, Medicare, federal unemployment tax, and state unemployment tax. Do not include federal or state income taxes withheld.

Note: Include any license fees, employer payroll taxes, and any business personal property taxes required in your area. Don't include the property taxes on your home here; those are entered on **Form 8829**.

Line 24: Travel, Meals, and Entertainment

Calculate the deductible total of your travel, meals, and entertainment expenses below.

Business travel expenses (line 24a)   _____

Business meals and entertainment* (line 24b)   + _____

Deductible travel, meals, and entertainment expenses   = _____

* IRS rules only allow you to decuct 50% of meals eaten away from home.

Note: For travel expenses (line 24a), you may include any expenses for lodging, airfare, bus or train fare, and vehicle rental on trips that were primarily for your business. For meals and entertainment (line 24b), include only (1) meals that you ate away from your home when on a business trip; and (2) meals that you ate with a client and paid for. Do not include the cost of any food or meals for the children in your care, whether at home or away from home. You will enter those food expenses in Part V.

Line 25: Utilities

If you provided child care in a building that was not your home last year, enter the total you paid for the utilities in that building. Most family child care providers should leave this line blank and enter their home utilities on **Form 8829** instead.

Deductible utilities expenses   _____

Line 26: Wages

If you paid any wages to employees (including members of your family) last year, enter the gross wages that you paid. You may report the employee's share of the Social Security, Medicare, and state taxes that you withheld either here or on line 23.

Deductible wages expenses   _____

Note: Many family child care providers mistakenly believe that they don't have to withhold payroll taxes if they hire someone for only a few days a year. This isn't true; for more information, see the 2018 *Tax Workbook and Organizer.*

Line 27: Other Expenses (from Part V)

Add up all your business expenses the back of **Schedule C**. Your tax professional will enter these expenses on the blank lines in Part V of **Schedule C**. Since there are no rules about how to organize your expenses, you can group the items on this list any way you like; however, it is best to show itemized categories (a single large deduction is more likely to attract the attention of the IRS). Remember, you can now deduct all expenses under $2,500 (with the exceptions of a home, home improvement, or home addition), directly onto **Schedule C**, without using **Form 4562**. For expenses that cost more than $2,500, put them on **Form 4562**, line 14. I suggest that family child care providers use the following categories.

Food (food expenses deduction from worksheet 14, page 45)   _____

Your total shared business and personal **toy expenses**   _____

Your Time-Space percentage   X _____

Business portion of toy expenses   = _____

Your 100% toy expenses   + _____

Deductible toy expenses   = _____

Your total shared business and personal
household expenses (yard expenses, safety items, tools)   _____

Your Time-Space percentage   X _____

Business portion of household expenses   = _____

Your 100% household expenses   + _____

Deductible household expenses   = _____

Your total shared business and personal
cleaning supply expenses   _____

Your Time-Space percentage   X _____

Business portion of cleaning supply expenses   = _____

Your 100% cleaning supply expenses   + _____

Deductible cleaning supply expenses   = _____

Your total shared business and personal
activity expenses (field trips, parties, special activities)   _____

Your Time-Space percentage   X _____

Business portion of activity expenses   = _____

Your 100% activity expenses   + _____

Deductible activity expenses   = _____

Your total shared business and personal **de minimis equipment
expenses** (those expenses that qualify for the $2,500 rule)   _____

Your Time-Space percentage   X _____

Business portion of de minimis equipment expenses   = _____

Your 100% de minimis equipment expenses   + _____

Deductible de minimis equipment expenses   = _____

Other* (describe): _____

Your total shared business and personal other expenses   _____

Your Time-Space percentage	x	_____
Business portion of other expenses	=	_____
Your 100% other expenses	+	_____
Deductible other expenses	=	_____
Deductible other expenses (sum of above total expenses)		_____

* If you have a lot of items under this heading, be prepared to show your tax professional your records to support your deduction.

Note: Include on the preceding list any other business expenses you aren't sure where to enter. For a list of hundreds of items that you may deduct, see the *Record-Keeping Guide*.

There may be occasions when you use an item a greater percentage of the time in your business than is reflected in your Time-Space percentage. If this is the case, you have the option of claiming an actual business-use percentage. To use this method, you must have kept a record showing how you calculated your actual business-use percentage. For details on how to calculate this, see the *Record-Keeping Guide*. Before using this method, consult with your tax professional.

Review Checklist for Schedule C

After your tax professional has completed all the forms for your tax return, you should review them before they are submitted to the IRS. Compare the numbers on your **Schedule C** to this section of the organizer and ask your tax professional to explain any discrepancies. Make sure you understand how each number on this form was calculated and keep detailed records of those calculations with your tax files for this year.

When reviewing **Schedule C**, first go through the checklist below and then go back and double-check all your deductions, as described in the next section.

PARTS I AND III

❒ As a rule, family child care providers do not have any returns, allowances, or cost of goods sold. So lines 2–4 in Part I and all of Part III (Cost of Goods Sold) should be left blank.

PART II

❒ You aren't required to list any of your deductions on a particular line. It doesn't matter if your tax professional wants to put your calculator under the Office Expenses (line 18) or under Supplies (line 22). You just need to know which deductions went on which line so you can produce receipts to support your return if you are ever audited.

❒ On line 9, make sure you have claimed the business portion of your car loan interest and personal property tax. Although this is often missed, you are always entitled to this deduction, even if you use the standard mileage rate method. To make sure you have properly included this business portion, check your numbers in worksheet 9 and worksheet 10 in this organizer.

❒ If you used the actual vehicle expenses method for a vehicle, you can also claim depreciation for that vehicle. Check that your tax professional has entered that deduction on line 25 or 26 of **Form 4562**. (You can't claim this deduction if you use the standard mileage rate method.)

❑ On line 13, make sure your tax professional has entered the depreciation deduction calculated on **Form 4562**. (In addition to depreciating your vehicle and business property, you are entitled to claim depreciation on all the household furniture and appliances that you are using in your business.)

❑ Check lines 8–26 to see if the totals on any of the lines are significantly larger than the others. If there is a larger total, you may want to break it into smaller categories and list them separately on line 27. This will provide better disclosure of your deductions and may reduce your risk of an audit.

❑ If you provide child care in a building that isn't your home, check that your tax professional has entered your home expenses (property tax, mortgage interest, homeowners insurance, home rent, utilities, home repairs, and home depreciation) on **Schedule C** instead of filing **Form 8829**.

❑ Check that your tax professional has transferred the amount on **Schedule C**, line 29, to **Form 8829**, line 8.

❑ Check that your tax professional has transferred the amount on **Form 8829**, line 35, to **Schedule C**, line 30. Only use the Simplified Method to claim house expenses if you are sure they are higher than your **Form 8829** expenses. See the instructions to **Form 8829** for more details on the Simplified Method.

❑ Check the net profit or loss for your business shown on **Schedule C**, line 31. It's okay to show a loss once or twice every five years, but if you have a loss more often than this, you may attract the attention of the IRS. If you do have a large loss, talk with your tax professional and let him know if you expect to show further losses in upcoming years.

What should your profit be on **Schedule C**, line 31? In a national study, the average family child care provider's total expenses (line 28 plus line 30) were 58% of line 7. (For higher-income providers this number dropped to 42%.) The average expenses shown on line 35 of **Form 8829** were 20% of line 7 on **Schedule C**. (For more information about this study, see the *Record-Keeping Guide*.)

Your situation may not be comparable to these average numbers. If your tax return is very different from this, you may want to ask your tax professional if there is an explanation.

PART IV

❑ If you used a vehicle in your business and are filing **Form 4562**, then Part IV of **Schedule C**, Information on Your Vehicle, should be left blank. Instead, check that your tax professional has entered your vehicle information in Part V of **Form 4562**.

❑ Part IV of **Schedule C** should be completed only if you used a vehicle in your business and aren't filing **Form 4562**.

Part V

❏ Compare your deduction for food expenses in Part V with the Food Program income you reported on line 6 of **Schedule C**. If you received the higher Food Program rate (Tier I) but served extra snacks that weren't reimbursed by the Food Program, your deduction for food expenses should be at least several hundred dollars higher than the amount on line 6. If you received the lower Food Program rate (Tier II), your deduction for food expenses should be at least twice as much as the amount on line 6.

Double-Check All Your Deductions

When you review your completed **Schedule C**, it's critical that you double-check all the deductions on that form and make sure they have been calculated properly.

- If an item was used 100% for your business, you should be deducting 100% of its cost.

- If an item was used only partly for your business, you should be deducting only part of its cost, usually your Time-Space percentage.

In particular, check the following lines on **Schedule C**, as these are the categories that are most likely to be calculated incorrectly:

- Line 18: Office Expenses

- Line 21: Repairs and Maintenance

- Line 22: Supplies

- Line 27: Other Expenses

For example, let's say that your tax professional has $437 listed on line 22. That amount might represent

- 100% of the cost of all your supplies (business and personal);

- 100% of the cost of your business supplies only; or

- 100% of the cost of your business supplies plus the Time-Space percentage of your shared business and personal supplies.

Do you know which it is? Check **Schedule C**, line 22, in this organizer and see if $437 is the same number that you entered there; if it is, check your own assumptions and calculations to make sure that this deduction is correct.

If $437 isn't the number you listed on line 22, you need to find out how this amount was calculated and why it is different from your number. Ask your tax professional to show you how she calculated this deduction, and check her assumptions carefully. If her figures are correct, rewrite the entries in this organizer and attach a copy of her calculations to this book.

If you don't double-check your deductions on **Schedule C**, you may not be paying the taxes that you actually owe. Also, if you are ever audited, you will have to defend every deduction on **Schedule C** and show how it was calculated. This will be relatively easy if the numbers on that form are the same as those you entered in this organizer (or if you have copies of your tax professional's calculations). Otherwise, you may have a serious problem.

Final Review

After your tax professional has completed all the forms for your tax return, you should review them before they are submitted to the IRS. Listed below are the points you should make sure to check on **Schedule SE** and **Form 1040**.

Review Checklist for Schedule SE

❐ If you report more than $400 profit on **Schedule C**, line 31, you must file **Schedule SE**. Your tax professional will use this form to calculate your self-employment or Social Security tax.

❐ Check that your tax professional has entered your profit from **Schedule C**, line 31, on line 2 of **Schedule SE**.

❐ Line 5 of **Schedule SE** shows the total Social Security or self-employment tax that you owe for last year. Check that this number is also entered on **Form 1040**, line 56.

❐ Line 6 of **Schedule SE** shows one-half of your self-employment tax. Check that this number is also entered on **Form 1040**, line 27, where it will reduce your federal taxable income.

Review Checklist for Form 1040

❐ On **Form 1040**, line 12, check that your tax professional has entered your net profit or loss from **Schedule C**, line 31.

❐ On line 27, check that your tax professional has entered one-half of the Social Security tax that was calculated on **Schedule SE**. (This line will reduce your taxes.)

❐ If you filed quarterly estimated tax payments (using **Form 1040-ES**), check that your tax professional entered all the quarterly payments that you made on line 62.

Double-Check All Your Tax Forms

Before your tax professional submits your tax return, take the time to do a final check:

❐ Double-check all the calculations on your tax forms.

❐ Check the Social Security numbers for you and your spouse to make sure they are correct.

❐ Both you and your spouse should sign your **Form 1040** if you are married filing jointly.

After Submitting Your Return

Save Your Records

❐ Keep copies of your receipts and business records, including your notations in this organizer, for at least three years after submitting your tax return.

❐ Keep copies of the receipts and records for the items you are depreciating for the depreciation period plus three years.

❑ Ask your tax professional for copies of any worksheets or other materials that he prepared while doing your tax return. If you get audited and your tax professional isn't available, you will need these records to help defend your return.

❑ Keep copies of all your tax returns for your lifetime.

❑ Put your tax records in a sealed plastic storage box (to protect them from water damage) and put the box in a safe place.

If You Discover an Error Later

❑ If you discover a mistake on your tax return after you have filed it, you can use **Form 1040X** to amend your return and correct the error. You have up to three years after filing a return to amend it. The 2018 *Tax Workbook and Organizer* includes a chapter on amending your return.

❑ If you find an error on an earlier tax return, discuss with your tax professional the best way to handle it.

How and When Should You Depreciate an Item?

Step 1: Does It Cost More Than $2,500?

This rule is effective for 2015 and after. If the answer is yes, go to step 2. If no, deduct it in one year. If it's part of a home improvement, see step 4.

Step 2: Is It a Repair?

In 2014, the definition of repair was expanded. If the answer is yes, deduct it in one year, regardless of the cost. If no, go to step 3.

Step 3: Choose a Depreciation Category

Office equipment (computer, printer, copy machine)

Personal property (furniture, appliances, play equipment)

Land improvement (fence, patio, driveway)

Home improvement (house, deck, new addition, major remodeling)

Step 4: Follow the Directions for Each Depreciation Category

Office equipment:

- Costing less than $2,500: deduct in one year and attach statement to your tax return
- Costing more than $2,500:
  - ◦ If you use less than 50% for your business, depreciate over five years
  - ◦ If you use 50% or more for your business
    - Use the Section 179 rule, or
    - Use the 100% bonus depreciation rule and deduct in one year, or
    - Depreciate over five years

Personal property:

- Costing less than $2,500: deduct in one year and attach statement to your tax return
- Costing more than $2,500:
  - ◦ Use 100% bonus depreciation rule and deduct in one year, or
  - ◦ Depreciate over seven years
- If you use 50% or more for your business
  - ◦ Can use the Section 179 rule

Land improvement:

- Costing less than $2,500: deduct in one year and attach statement to your tax return
- Costing more than $2,500:
  - ◦ Use the 100% bonus depreciation rule and deduct in one year
  - ◦ Does the Safe Harbor for Small Taxpayers rule apply (effective 2014 and after)?
    - If yes, deduct in one year

- If no, use the 100% bonus depreciation rule and deduct in one year, or depreciate over 15 years

Home improvement:

- Costing less than $2,500: deduct in one year and attach statement to your tax return
- Costing more than $2,500:
  - Does the Safe Harbor for Small Taxpayers rule apply (rule effective 2014 and after)?
    - If yes, deduct in one year
    - If no, depreciate over 39 years, or if used more than 50% for business, use the Section 179 rule

Home:

- Depreciate over 39 years

MEAL FORM Week of ____________ 2018

Child	Mon	Tue	Wed	Thu	Fri	Sat	Sun	Totals
	Bkst ___ Lun ___ Din ___ Sn1 ___ Sn2 ___ Sn3 ___	Bkst ___ Lun ___ Din ___ Sn1 ___ Sn2 ___ Sn3 ___	Bkst ___ Lun ___ Din ___ Sn1 ___ Sn2 ___ Sn3 ___	Bkst ___ Lun ___ Din ___ Sn1 ___ Sn2 ___ Sn3 ___	Bkst ___ Lun ___ Din ___ Sn1 ___ Sn2 ___ Sn3 ___	Bkst ___ Lun ___ Din ___ Sn1 ___ Sn2 ___ Sn3 ___	Bkst ___ Lun ___ Din ___ Sn1 ___ Sn2 ___ Sn3 ___	B ___ L ___ D ___ S ___
	Bkst ___ Lun ___ Din ___ Sn1 ___ Sn2 ___ Sn3 ___	Bkst ___ Lun ___ Din ___ Sn1 ___ Sn2 ___ Sn3 ___	Bkst ___ Lun ___ Din ___ Sn1 ___ Sn2 ___ Sn3 ___	Bkst ___ Lun ___ Din ___ Sn1 ___ Sn2 ___ Sn3 ___	Bkst ___ Lun ___ Din ___ Sn1 ___ Sn2 ___ Sn3 ___	Bkst ___ Lun ___ Din ___ Sn1 ___ Sn2 ___ Sn3 ___	Bkst ___ Lun ___ Din ___ Sn1 ___ Sn2 ___ Sn3 ___	B ___ L ___ D ___ S ___
	Bkst ___ Lun ___ Din ___ Sn1 ___ Sn2 ___ Sn3 ___	Bkst ___ Lun ___ Din ___ Sn1 ___ Sn2 ___ Sn3 ___	Bkst ___ Lun ___ Din ___ Sn1 ___ Sn2 ___ Sn3 ___	Bkst ___ Lun ___ Din ___ Sn1 ___ Sn2 ___ Sn3 ___	Bkst ___ Lun ___ Din ___ Sn1 ___ Sn2 ___ Sn3 ___	Bkst ___ Lun ___ Din ___ Sn1 ___ Sn2 ___ Sn3 ___	Bkst ___ Lun ___ Din ___ Sn1 ___ Sn2 ___ Sn3 ___	B ___ L ___ D ___ S ___
	Bkst ___ Lun ___ Din ___ Sn1 ___ Sn2 ___ Sn3 ___	Bkst ___ Lun ___ Din ___ Sn1 ___ Sn2 ___ Sn3 ___	Bkst ___ Lun ___ Din ___ Sn1 ___ Sn2 ___ Sn3 ___	Bkst ___ Lun ___ Din ___ Sn1 ___ Sn2 ___ Sn3 ___	Bkst ___ Lun ___ Din ___ Sn1 ___ Sn2 ___ Sn3 ___	Bkst ___ Lun ___ Din ___ Sn1 ___ Sn2 ___ Sn3 ___	Bkst ___ Lun ___ Din ___ Sn1 ___ Sn2 ___ Sn3 ___	B ___ L ___ D ___ S ___
	Bkst ___ Lun ___ Din ___ Sn1 ___ Sn2 ___ Sn3 ___	Bkst ___ Lun ___ Din ___ Sn1 ___ Sn2 ___ Sn3 ___	Bkst ___ Lun ___ Din ___ Sn1 ___ Sn2 ___ Sn3 ___	Bkst ___ Lun ___ Din ___ Sn1 ___ Sn2 ___ Sn3 ___	Bkst ___ Lun ___ Din ___ Sn1 ___ Sn2 ___ Sn3 ___	Bkst ___ Lun ___ Din ___ Sn1 ___ Sn2 ___ Sn3 ___	Bkst ___ Lun ___ Din ___ Sn1 ___ Sn2 ___ Sn3 ___	B ___ L ___ D ___ S ___
	Bkst ___ Lun ___ Din ___ Sn1 ___ Sn2 ___ Sn3 ___	Bkst ___ Lun ___ Din ___ Sn1 ___ Sn2 ___ Sn3 ___	Bkst ___ Lun ___ Din ___ Sn1 ___ Sn2 ___ Sn3 ___	Bkst ___ Lun ___ Din ___ Sn1 ___ Sn2 ___ Sn3 ___	Bkst ___ Lun ___ Din ___ Sn1 ___ Sn2 ___ Sn3 ___	Bkst ___ Lun ___ Din ___ Sn1 ___ Sn2 ___ Sn3 ___	Bkst ___ Lun ___ Din ___ Sn1 ___ Sn2 ___ Sn3 ___	B ___ L ___ D ___ S ___

Child	Mon	Tue	Wed	Thu	Fri	Sat	Sun	Totals
	Bkst ___ Lun ___ Din ___ Sn1 ___ Sn2 ___ Sn3 ___	Bkst ___ Lun ___ Din ___ Sn1 ___ Sn2 ___ Sn3 ___	Bkst ___ Lun ___ Din ___ Sn1 ___ Sn2 ___ Sn3 ___	Bkst ___ Lun ___ Din ___ Sn1 ___ Sn2 ___ Sn3 ___	Bkst ___ Lun ___ Din ___ Sn1 ___ Sn2 ___ Sn3 ___	Bkst ___ Lun ___ Din ___ Sn1 ___ Sn2 ___ Sn3 ___	Bkst ___ Lun ___ Din ___ Sn1 ___ Sn2 ___ Sn3 ___	B ___ L ___ D ___ S ___
	Bkst ___ Lun ___ Din ___ Sn1 ___ Sn2 ___ Sn3 ___	Bkst ___ Lun ___ Din ___ Sn1 ___ Sn2 ___ Sn3 ___	Bkst ___ Lun ___ Din ___ Sn1 ___ Sn2 ___ Sn3 ___	Bkst ___ Lun ___ Din ___ Sn1 ___ Sn2 ___ Sn3 ___	Bkst ___ Lun ___ Din ___ Sn1 ___ Sn2 ___ Sn3 ___	Bkst ___ Lun ___ Din ___ Sn1 ___ Sn2 ___ Sn3 ___	Bkst ___ Lun ___ Din ___ Sn1 ___ Sn2 ___ Sn3 ___	B ___ L ___ D ___ S ___
	Bkst ___ Lun ___ Din ___ Sn1 ___ Sn2 ___ Sn3 ___	Bkst ___ Lun ___ Din ___ Sn1 ___ Sn2 ___ Sn3 ___	Bkst ___ Lun ___ Din ___ Sn1 ___ Sn2 ___ Sn3 ___	Bkst ___ Lun ___ Din ___ Sn1 ___ Sn2 ___ Sn3 ___	Bkst ___ Lun ___ Din ___ Sn1 ___ Sn2 ___ Sn3 ___	Bkst ___ Lun ___ Din ___ Sn1 ___ Sn2 ___ Sn3 ___	Bkst ___ Lun ___ Din ___ Sn1 ___ Sn2 ___ Sn3 ___	B ___ L ___ D ___ S ___
	Bkst ___ Lun ___ Din ___ Sn1 ___ Sn2 ___ Sn3 ___	Bkst ___ Lun ___ Din ___ Sn1 ___ Sn2 ___ Sn3 ___	Bkst ___ Lun ___ Din ___ Sn1 ___ Sn2 ___ Sn3 ___	Bkst ___ Lun ___ Din ___ Sn1 ___ Sn2 ___ Sn3 ___	Bkst ___ Lun ___ Din ___ Sn1 ___ Sn2 ___ Sn3 ___	Bkst ___ Lun ___ Din ___ Sn1 ___ Sn2 ___ Sn3 ___	Bkst ___ Lun ___ Din ___ Sn1 ___ Sn2 ___ Sn3 ___	B ___ L ___ D ___ S ___
	Bkst ___ Lun ___ Din ___ Sn1 ___ Sn2 ___ Sn3 ___	Bkst ___ Lun ___ Din ___ Sn1 ___ Sn2 ___ Sn3 ___	Bkst ___ Lun ___ Din ___ Sn1 ___ Sn2 ___ Sn3 ___	Bkst ___ Lun ___ Din ___ Sn1 ___ Sn2 ___ Sn3 ___	Bkst ___ Lun ___ Din ___ Sn1 ___ Sn2 ___ Sn3 ___	Bkst ___ Lun ___ Din ___ Sn1 ___ Sn2 ___ Sn3 ___	Bkst ___ Lun ___ Din ___ Sn1 ___ Sn2 ___ Sn3 ___	B ___ L ___ D ___ S ___
	Bkst ___ Lun ___ Din ___ Sn1 ___ Sn2 ___ Sn3 ___	Bkst ___ Lun ___ Din ___ Sn1 ___ Sn2 ___ Sn3 ___	Bkst ___ Lun ___ Din ___ Sn1 ___ Sn2 ___ Sn3 ___	Bkst ___ Lun ___ Din ___ Sn1 ___ Sn2 ___ Sn3 ___	Bkst ___ Lun ___ Din ___ Sn1 ___ Sn2 ___ Sn3 ___	Bkst ___ Lun ___ Din ___ Sn1 ___ Sn2 ___ Sn3 ___	Bkst ___ Lun ___ Din ___ Sn1 ___ Sn2 ___ Sn3 ___	B ___ L ___ D ___ S ___

Place a check mark (✓) next to each meal or snack you serve. Do not count meals served to your own children. If you are on the Food Program, use this form to track your nonreimbursed meals only. Add the reimbursed meals from your monthly claim forms and the nonreimbursed meals from this form together, and put the totals on the year-end meal tally on page 59. If you are not on the Food Program, use this form to track all your meals, and put the totals on the year-end meal tally on page 59.

Make copies of this form for each week of the year. If you have six or fewer children in your program, you can use one form for two weeks. You can download this form at the Redleaf Press website. Go to www.redleafpress.org, and find the page for the *Redleaf Calendar-Keeper 2018*. There will be a link to this form.

Weekly Totals

Breakfasts ________ Dinners ________

Lunches ________ Snacks ________

YEAR-END MEAL TALLY

If you are not on the Food Program, enter all meals and snacks in the column labeled "Number Not Reimbursed by Food Program."

	Breakfasts		Lunches		Dinners		Snacks	
	Number Reimbursed by Food Program	Number Not Reimbursed by Food Program	Number Reimbursed by Food Program	Number Not Reimbursed by Food Program	Number Reimbursed by Food Program	Number Not Reimbursed by Food Program	Number Reimbursed by Food Program	Number Not Reimbursed by Food Program
January								
February								
March								
April								
May								
June								
July								
August								
September								
October								
November								
December								
TOTAL								

2018 Standard Meal Allowance Rate*

Number of Breakfasts _____ X $1.31 = $ _____
Number of Lunches _____ X $2.46 = $ _____
Number of Dinners _____ X $2.46 = $ _____
Number of Snacks _____ X $0.73 = $ _____
Total Food Deductions $ _____ †

Do not report any meals served to your own children (even if they are reimbursed by the Food Program).

* The IRS standard meal allowance rate for 2018 used in these calculations is based on the Tier I rate as of January 1, 2018. This rate is used for all meals and snacks served throughout 2018, even though the Tier I rate goes up every July. All providers, whether on Tier I or Tier II (and all providers not on the Food Program), will use the rates listed.

† Enter this amount on Form 1040 Schedule C, Part V. Be sure to enter any reimbursements from the Food Program (with the exception of reimbursements for your own children) as income on Form 1040 Schedule C, line 6.

Form 8829

Department of the Treasury Internal Revenue Service (99)

Expenses for Business Use of Your Home

▶ **File only with Schedule C (Form 1040). Use a separate Form 8829 for each home you used for business during the year.**

▶ **Go to *www.irs.gov/Form8829* for instructions and the latest information.**

OMB No. 1545-0074

2018

Attachment Sequence No. **176**

Name(s) of proprietor(s)

Your social security number

Part I Part of Your Home Used for Business

1	Area used regularly and exclusively for business, regularly for daycare, or for storage of inventory or product samples (see instructions)	**1**	
2	Total area of home	**2**	
3	Divide line 1 by line 2. Enter the result as a percentage	**3**	%

For daycare facilities not used exclusively for business, go to line 4. All others, go to line 7.

4	Multiply days used for daycare during year by hours used per day	**4**	hr.
5	Total hours available for use during the year (365 days x 24 hours) (see instructions)	**5**	hr.
6	Divide line 4 by line 5. Enter the result as a decimal amount	**6**	.
7	Business percentage. For daycare facilities not used exclusively for business, multiply line 6 by line 3 (enter the result as a percentage). All others, enter the amount from line 3 ▶	**7**	%

Part II Figure Your Allowable Deduction

8	Enter the amount from Schedule C, line 29, **plus** any gain derived from the business use of your home, **minus** any loss from the trade or business not derived from the business use of your home (see instructions)		**8**	

See instructions for columns (a) and (b) before completing lines 9–22.

		(a) Direct expenses	(b) Indirect expenses		
9	Casualty losses (see instructions)	**9**			
10	Deductible mortgage interest (see instructions)	**10**			
11	Real estate taxes (see instructions)	**11**			
12	Add lines 9, 10, and 11	**12**			
13	Multiply line 12, column (b), by line 7		**13**		
14	Add line 12, column (a), and line 13			**14**	
15	Subtract line 14 from line 8. If zero or less, enter -0-			**15**	
16	Excess mortgage interest (see instructions)	**16**			
17	Excess real estate taxes (see instructions)	**17**			
18	Insurance	**18**			
19	Rent	**19**			
20	Repairs and maintenance	**20**			
21	Utilities	**21**			
22	Other expenses (see instructions)	**22**			
23	Add lines 16 through 22	**23**			
24	Multiply line 23, column (b), by line 7		**24**		
25	Carryover of prior year operating expenses (see instructions)		**25**		
26	Add line 23, column (a), line 24, and line 25			**26**	
27	Allowable operating expenses. Enter the **smaller** of line 15 or line 26			**27**	
28	Limit on excess casualty losses and depreciation. Subtract line 27 from line 15			**28**	
29	Excess casualty losses (see instructions)		**29**		
30	Depreciation of your home from line 42 below		**30**		
31	Carryover of prior year excess casualty losses and depreciation (see instructions)		**31**		
32	Add lines 29 through 31			**32**	
33	Allowable excess casualty losses and depreciation. Enter the **smaller** of line 28 or line 32			**33**	
34	Add lines 14, 27, and 33			**34**	
35	Casualty loss portion, if any, from lines 14 and 33. Carry amount to **Form 4684** (see instructions)			**35**	
36	**Allowable expenses for business use of your home.** Subtract line 35 from line 34. Enter here and on Schedule C, line 30. If your home was used for more than one business, see instructions ▶			**36**	

Part III Depreciation of Your Home

37	Enter the **smaller** of your home's adjusted basis or its fair market value (see instructions)	**37**	
38	Value of land included on line 37	**38**	
39	Basis of building. Subtract line 38 from line 37	**39**	
40	Business basis of building. Multiply line 39 by line 7	**40**	
41	Depreciation percentage (see instructions)	**41**	%
42	Depreciation allowable (see instructions). Multiply line 40 by line 41. Enter here and on line 30 above	**42**	

Part IV Carryover of Unallowed Expenses to 2019

43	Operating expenses. Subtract line 27 from line 26. If less than zero, enter -0-	**43**	
44	Excess casualty losses and depreciation. Subtract line 33 from line 32. If less than zero, enter -0-	**44**	

For Paperwork Reduction Act Notice, see your tax return instructions. Cat. No. 13232M Form **8829** (2018)

Form **4562**	**Depreciation and Amortization**	OMB No. 1545-0172
Department of the Treasury Internal Revenue Service (99)	**(Including Information on Listed Property)** ▶ Attach to your tax return. ▶ Go to *www.irs.gov/Form4562* for instructions and the latest information.	**2018** Attachment Sequence No. **179**

Name(s) shown on return	Business or activity to which this form relates	Identifying number

Part I Election To Expense Certain Property Under Section 179
Note: If you have any listed property, complete Part V before you complete Part I.

1	Maximum amount (see instructions)	**1**	
2	Total cost of section 179 property placed in service (see instructions)	**2**	
3	Threshold cost of section 179 property before reduction in limitation (see instructions)	**3**	
4	Reduction in limitation. Subtract line 3 from line 2. If zero or less, enter -0-	**4**	
5	Dollar limitation for tax year. Subtract line 4 from line 1. If zero or less, enter -0-. If married filing separately, see instructions	**5**	

6	(a) Description of property	(b) Cost (business use only)	(c) Elected cost

7	Listed property. Enter the amount from line 29 . . . . **7**		
8	Total elected cost of section 179 property. Add amounts in column (c), lines 6 and 7	**8**	
9	Tentative deduction. Enter the **smaller** of line 5 or line 8	**9**	
10	Carryover of disallowed deduction from line 13 of your 2017 Form 4562	**10**	
11	Business income limitation. Enter the smaller of business income (not less than zero) or line 5. See instructions	**11**	
12	Section 179 expense deduction. Add lines 9 and 10, but don't enter more than line 11	**12**	
13	Carryover of disallowed deduction to 2019. Add lines 9 and 10, less line 12 ▶ **13**		

Note: Don't use Part II or Part III below for listed property. Instead, use Part V.

Part II Special Depreciation Allowance and Other Depreciation (Don't include listed property. See instructions.)

14	Special depreciation allowance for qualified property (other than listed property) placed in service during the tax year. See instructions	**14**	
15	Property subject to section 168(f)(1) election	**15**	
16	Other depreciation (including ACRS)	**16**	

Part III MACRS Depreciation (Don't include listed property. See instructions.)

Section A

17	MACRS deductions for assets placed in service in tax years beginning before 2018	**17**	
18	If you are electing to group any assets placed in service during the tax year into one or more general asset accounts, check here ▶ ☐		

Section B—Assets Placed in Service During 2018 Tax Year Using the General Depreciation System

(a) Classification of property	(b) Month and year placed in service	(c) Basis for depreciation (business/investment use only—see instructions)	(d) Recovery period	(e) Convention	(f) Method	(g) Depreciation deduction
19a 3-year property						
b 5-year property						
c 7-year property						
d 10-year property						
e 15-year property						
f 20-year property						
g 25-year property			25 yrs.		S/L	
h Residential rental property			27.5 yrs.	MM	S/L	
			27.5 yrs.	MM	S/L	
i Nonresidential real property			39 yrs.	MM	S/L	
				MM	S/L	

Section C—Assets Placed in Service During 2018 Tax Year Using the Alternative Depreciation System

(a) Classification of property	(b)	(c)	(d)	(e)	(f)	(g)
20a Class life					S/L	
b 12-year			12 yrs.		S/L	
c 30-year			30 yrs.	MM	S/L	
d 40-year			40 yrs.	MM	S/L	

Part IV Summary (See instructions.)

21	Listed property. Enter amount from line 28	**21**	
22	**Total.** Add amounts from line 12, lines 14 through 17, lines 19 and 20 in column (g), and line 21. Enter here and on the appropriate lines of your return. Partnerships and S corporations—see instructions	**22**	
23	For assets shown above and placed in service during the current year, enter the portion of the basis attributable to section 263A costs **23**		

For Paperwork Reduction Act Notice, see separate instructions.   Cat. No. 12906N   Form **4562** (2018)

Form 4562 (2018)   Page **2**

Part V | **Listed Property** (Include automobiles, certain other vehicles, certain aircraft, and property used for entertainment, recreation, or amusement.)

Note: For any vehicle for which you are using the standard mileage rate or deducting lease expense, complete **only** 24a, 24b, columns (a) through (c) of Section A, all of Section B, and Section C if applicable.

Section A—Depreciation and Other Information (Caution: See the instructions for limits for passenger automobiles.**)**

24a Do you have evidence to support the business/investment use claimed? ☐ **Yes** ☐ **No**   **24b** If "Yes," is the evidence written? ☐ **Yes** ☐ **No**

(a) Type of property (list vehicles first)	(b) Date placed in service	(c) Business/ investment use percentage	(d) Cost or other basis	(e) Basis for depreciation (business/investment use only)	(f) Recovery period	(g) Method/ Convention	(h) Depreciation deduction	(i) Elected section 179 cost
25 Special depreciation allowance for qualified listed property placed in service during the tax year and used more than 50% in a qualified business use. See instructions .				**25**				
26 Property used more than 50% in a qualified business use:								
		%						
		%						
		%						
27 Property used 50% or less in a qualified business use:								
		%				S/L –		
		%				S/L –		
		%				S/L –		
28 Add amounts in column (h), lines 25 through 27. Enter here and on line 21, page 1 .						**28**		
29 Add amounts in column (i), line 26. Enter here and on line 7, page 1							**29**	

Section B—Information on Use of Vehicles

Complete this section for vehicles used by a sole proprietor, partner, or other "more than 5% owner," or related person. If you provided vehicles to your employees, first answer the questions in Section C to see if you meet an exception to completing this section for those vehicles.

		(a) Vehicle 1		(b) Vehicle 2		(c) Vehicle 3		(d) Vehicle 4		(e) Vehicle 5		(f) Vehicle 6	
30	Total business/investment miles driven during the year (**don't** include commuting miles) .												
31	Total commuting miles driven during the year												
32	Total other personal (noncommuting) miles driven												
33	Total miles driven during the year. Add lines 30 through 32												
34	Was the vehicle available for personal use during off-duty hours?	Yes	No	Yes	No	Yes	No	Yes	No	Yes	No	Yes	No
35	Was the vehicle used primarily by a more than 5% owner or related person? . .												
36	Is another vehicle available for personal use?												

Section C—Questions for Employers Who Provide Vehicles for Use by Their Employees

Answer these questions to determine if you meet an exception to completing Section B for vehicles used by employees who **aren't** more than 5% owners or related persons. See instructions.

		Yes	No
37	Do you maintain a written policy statement that prohibits all personal use of vehicles, including commuting, by your employees?		
38	Do you maintain a written policy statement that prohibits personal use of vehicles, except commuting, by your employees? See the instructions for vehicles used by corporate officers, directors, or 1% or more owners . .		
39	Do you treat all use of vehicles by employees as personal use?		
40	Do you provide more than five vehicles to your employees, obtain information from your employees about the use of the vehicles, and retain the information received?		
41	Do you meet the requirements concerning qualified automobile demonstration use? See instructions. . . .		

Note: If your answer to 37, 38, 39, 40, or 41 is "Yes," don't complete Section B for the covered vehicles.

Part VI | **Amortization**

(a) Description of costs	(b) Date amortization begins	(c) Amortizable amount	(d) Code section	(e) Amortization period or percentage	(f) Amortization for this year
42 Amortization of costs that begins during your 2018 tax year (see instructions):					
43 Amortization of costs that began before your 2018 tax year **43**					
44 **Total.** Add amounts in column (f). See the instructions for where to report **44**					

Form **4562** (2018)

SCHEDULE C
(Form 1040)

Department of the Treasury
Internal Revenue Service (99)

Profit or Loss From Business
(Sole Proprietorship)

▶ Go to *www.irs.gov/ScheduleC* for instructions and the latest information.
▶ Attach to Form 1040, 1040NR, or 1041; partnerships generally must file Form 1065.

OMB No. 1545-0074

2018

Attachment
Sequence No. **09**

Name of proprietor

Social security number (SSN)

A	Principal business or profession, including product or service (see instructions)	B Enter code from instructions ▶
C	Business name. If no separate business name, leave blank.	D Employer ID number (EIN) (see instr.)

E   Business address (including suite or room no.) ▶
City, town or post office, state, and ZIP code

F   Accounting method: (1) ☐ Cash   (2) ☐ Accrual   (3) ☐ Other (specify) ▶

G   Did you "materially participate" in the operation of this business during 2018? If "No," see instructions for limit on losses   . ☐ Yes ☐ No

H   If you started or acquired this business during 2018, check here   . . . . ▶ ☐

I   Did you make any payments in 2018 that would require you to file Form(s) 1099? (see instructions) . . . . ☐ Yes ☐ No

J   If "Yes," did you or will you file required Forms 1099? . . . . ☐ Yes ☐ No

Part I   Income

1	Gross receipts or sales. See instructions for line 1 and check the box if this income was reported to you on Form W-2 and the "Statutory employee" box on that form was checked . . . . ▶ ☐	1	
2	Returns and allowances	2	
3	Subtract line 2 from line 1	3	
4	Cost of goods sold (from line 42)	4	
5	**Gross profit.** Subtract line 4 from line 3	5	
6	Other income, including federal and state gasoline or fuel tax credit or refund (see instructions)	6	
7	**Gross income.** Add lines 5 and 6 . . . . ▶	7	

Part II   Expenses. Enter expenses for business use of your home **only** on line 30.

8	Advertising	8		18	Office expense (see instructions)	18	
9	Car and truck expenses (see instructions). . . .	9		19	Pension and profit-sharing plans .	19	
				20	Rent or lease (see instructions):		
10	Commissions and fees .	10		a	Vehicles, machinery, and equipment	20a	
11	Contract labor (see instructions)	11		b	Other business property . . .	20b	
12	Depletion	12		21	Repairs and maintenance . . .	21	
13	Depreciation and section 179 expense deduction (not included in Part III) (see instructions).	13		22	Supplies (not included in Part III) .	22	
				23	Taxes and licenses	23	
				24	Travel and meals:		
14	Employee benefit programs (other than on line 19) . .	14		a	Travel.	24a	
15	Insurance (other than health)	15		b	Deductible meals (see instructions)	24b	
16	Interest (see instructions):			25	Utilities	25	
a	Mortgage (paid to banks, etc.)	16a		26	Wages (less employment credits) .	26	
b	Other	16b		27a	Other expenses (from line 48) . .	27a	
17	Legal and professional services	17		b	**Reserved for future use** . . .	27b	

28	**Total expenses** before expenses for business use of home. Add lines 8 through 27a . . . . . . ▶	28	
29	Tentative profit or (loss). Subtract line 28 from line 7	29	
30	Expenses for business use of your home. Do not report these expenses elsewhere. Attach Form 8829 unless using the simplified method (see instructions). **Simplified method filers only:** enter the total square footage of: (a) your home: _____ and (b) the part of your home used for business: _____ . Use the Simplified Method Worksheet in the instructions to figure the amount to enter on line 30	30	
31	**Net profit or (loss).** Subtract line 30 from line 29. • If a profit, enter on both **Schedule 1 (Form 1040), line 12** (or **Form 1040NR, line 13**) and on **Schedule SE, line 2**. (If you checked the box on line 1, see instructions). Estates and trusts, enter on **Form 1041, line 3**. • If a loss, you **must** go to line 32.	31	
32	If you have a loss, check the box that describes your investment in this activity (see instructions). • If you checked 32a, enter the loss on both **Schedule 1 (Form 1040), line 12** (or **Form 1040NR, line 13**) and on **Schedule SE, line 2**. (If you checked the box on line 1, see the line 31 instructions.) Estates and trusts, enter on **Form 1041, line 3**. • If you checked 32b, you **must** attach **Form 6198**. Your loss may be limited.	32a ☐ All investment is at risk. 32b ☐ Some investment is not at risk.	

For Paperwork Reduction Act Notice, see the separate instructions.   Cat. No. 11334P   Schedule C (Form 1040) 2018

Schedule C (Form 1040) 2018   Page **2**

Part III   Cost of Goods Sold (see instructions)

33   Method(s) used to value closing inventory: **a** ☐ Cost   **b** ☐ Lower of cost or market   **c** ☐ Other (attach explanation)

34   Was there any change in determining quantities, costs, or valuations between opening and closing inventory? If "Yes," attach explanation . . . . ☐ **Yes**   ☐ **No**

35 Inventory at beginning of year. If different from last year's closing inventory, attach explanation . . .	**35**	
36 Purchases less cost of items withdrawn for personal use	**36**	
37 Cost of labor. Do not include any amounts paid to yourself	**37**	
38 Materials and supplies	**38**	
39 Other costs	**39**	
40 Add lines 35 through 39	**40**	
41 Inventory at end of year	**41**	
42 **Cost of goods sold.** Subtract line 41 from line 40. Enter the result here and on line 4	**42**	

Part IV   Information on Your Vehicle. Complete this part **only** if you are claiming car or truck expenses on line 9 and are not required to file Form 4562 for this business. See the instructions for line 13 to find out if you must file Form 4562.

43   When did you place your vehicle in service for business purposes? (month, day, year) ▶ _____ / _____ / _____

44   Of the total number of miles you drove your vehicle during 2018, enter the number of miles you used your vehicle for:

   a Business _____   **b** Commuting (see instructions) _____   **c** Other _____

45   Was your vehicle available for personal use during off-duty hours? . . . . ☐ **Yes**   ☐ **No**

46   Do you (or your spouse) have another vehicle available for personal use?. . . . . ☐ **Yes**   ☐ **No**

47a   Do you have evidence to support your deduction? . . . . ☐ **Yes**   ☐ **No**

   b   If "Yes," is the evidence written? . . . . ☐ **Yes**   ☐ **No**

Part V   Other Expenses. List below business expenses not included on lines 8–26 or line 30.

_____		
_____		
_____		
_____		
_____		
_____		
_____		
_____		
48 **Total other expenses.** Enter here and on line 27a	**48**	